PEMBROKESHIRE VILLAGES

Geoffrey Davies

Published by Sigma Leisure – an imprint of
Sigma Press, Stobart House, Pontyclerc, Penybanc Road, Ammanford, Carmarthenshire SA18 3HP.

British Library Cataloguing in Publication Data
A CIP record for this book is available from the British Library.

ISBN: 978-1-85058-965-5

Typesetting and Design by: Sigma Press, Ammanford.

Cover photograph: St Domaels © Geoffrey Davies

Drawings: © Geoffrey Davies from old drawings by Thornhill Timmins

Printed by: TJ International Ltd, Padstow, Cornwall

Disclaimer: The information in this book is given in good faith and is believed to be correct at the time of publication. No responsibility is accepted by either the author or publisher for errors or omissions.

Contents

Introduction

Pembrokeshire is a beautiful county with a long coastline that boasts many fine beaches and spectacular cliff scenery coupled with a teeming wildlife. It is the site of Britain's only coastal National Park, established in 1952. The county's rivers play an important role. The Cych, Taf and Teifi form natural borders, while the Eastern and Western Cleddau rivers flow into Milford Haven. In the north, the River Gwaun carves an attractive valley. South Pembrokeshire is relatively flat and the highest point in the Preseli Mountain range in the north is 1742 feet.

The county is littered with Bronze and Iron Age religious, funerary and defensive sites. The bluestones at Stonehenge came from the Preseli Mountain range. It was long thought that the Romans had not ventured into Pembrokeshire, but Fenton suggested that there were the remains of a Roman villa near Wolfscastle and recent research has confirmed this. After the Romans left, Pembrokeshire became the centre for Christianity in Wales with St David's Cathedral becoming a place of pilgrimage and many local saints establishing churches.

Wales was divided among local tribes, only becoming united for short periods under powerful princes. The Welsh practice of gavelkind, whereby all children took an equal inheritance in their father's estate, meant that the country could not stay united.

In 1021 Olaf Haroldson, King of Norway, invaded Pembrokeshire and many of his Vikings settled along the coast, giving their names to places such as Skokholm and Grasholm Islands, Caldy, Ongull or Angel (a hook), Fishguard, Hasguard, Tenby (*Dane-bi*, Dane's house), Hakin (*Haakon*), Haroldston, Herbrandston, Thorney (Thorn *Ey* or Island), Haverford, (Havard's Fiord) and Orielton (Oriel-*ton*).

The county was divided into cantrefs under Welsh rule which were adopted as hundreds by the Normans. There were seven hundreds, namely Dewisland around St David's, Cemaes and Cilgerran in the north, Roose, Castlemartin and Narberth in the south and Dungleddy in the centre.

At the time of the Norman Conquest of England, Pembrokeshire, together with Carmarthenshire and Ceredigion, formed part of the kingdom of Deheubarth. Various leaders fought for control, often with the assistance of Irish or Viking armies. The Prince of Deheubarth,

Rhys ap Tewdwr, was killed at the Battle of Brecon in 1093 and his children Gruffydd and Nest and their offspring were subsequently to feature prominently in the history of Pembrokeshire, Ireland and Britain. In the latter part of the 12th century Gruffydd's youngest son Rhys, known as the Lord Rhys won back much of Deheubarth and was made Justicar of South Wales by Henry II. Rhys was not above using the marriage of his children to build powerful alliances, including with Normans, a practice continued by the prominent Welsh families for the next 700 years.

Historically the county has long had contact with Ireland and was, with Llancarfan in Glamorgan, the birthplace of Celtic Christianity. It was important as being on the direct route from London to Ireland, while Milford Haven is one of the world's finest natural harbours. It is not surprising then that William the Conqueror targeted the south of the county for settlement early in his reign. Pembroke Castle was one of the first Norman fortresses in Wales and as the castles were built, they were supported by an influx of Flemish settlers. Early in the 12th century the sea flooded a large part of Flanders and the inhabitants sought refuge across Europe. Henry I, whose mother was Flemish, and Henry II settled the immigrants in the southern part of Pembrokeshire in the Hundreds of Roose and Castlemartin. The Flemish language of the time was not dissimilar to the Anglo-Saxon then spoken in England. They, with the English who also came to South Pembrokeshire, were regarded by the Welsh as being "perjured, treacherous and in every respect immoral". The result has been an unusual but very precise division in the county known as the *Landsker*, south of which English is the dominant language, while to the north Welsh is the first language of the majority. Writing in 1809 Malkin described the county as having 144 parishes, 74 English and 64 Welsh with the remainder "speaking both languages or rather neither". Even today, there is a South Pembrokeshire dialect, a legacy of the Flemish settlers. The word *Landsker* is Norse in origin meaning border and this gives another insight into the county's history in that there were a large number of Viking settlements around the Pembrokeshire coast.

Place Names
The effects of the settlers can be seen in the place names. In the south there are numerous villages with the suffix *ton*, referring to a farm or settlement, with the name of the principal settler. Thus we have

Reynaldston, Rogerston and many others. As mentioned, the Vikings left their mark with names such as Freystrop as well as the islands of Skokholm and Gateholm, *holm* meaning island as in the Swedish capital of Stockholm. In the north of the county Welsh place names are more prevalent with the prefixes of *aber* and *llan* most common. *Aber* refers to the mouth of a river while *llan* denotes the site of a church. Celtic churches were traditionally built in the centre of a circular plot of land, known as a *llan*. It is believed that many of these sites were of pre-Christian religious significance.

In many instances, the spelling of place names has changed over the years, Richard Fenton's book written in 1810 shows Newgale as Newgall, Trecwn as Trecoon and Letterston as Lettardston. Many Welsh names have been anglicized and English names have changed to match local pronunciation. Where possible an explanation of the derivation of place names has been given in the text, but many are open to debate.

Language is not the only difference north and south of the *Landsker*. To the south the churches tend to have towers, while to the north the simple bellcote is the norm.

Many churches in Pembrokeshire have a 'squint', a window allowing the parishioners to the side of the nave to view the altar. The design of many medieval churches in the county meant that there were narrow chancel arches, preventing a clear view of the altar from the side pews in the nave. Squints were therefore built to provide a view. In some cases these were 'leper squints', allowing views of the altar from the outside of the church.

The history of Pembrokeshire is closely connected with a small number of wealthy families, whose names will crop up frequently throughout the pages of this book. Some are the descendants of the Norman knights, others, like the Philipps, trace their ancestry to the pre-Norman Welsh royal families, while others acquired lands through marriage to heiresses (e.g. Sir Alexander Campbell acquired the Stackpole Estate by his marriage to Elizabeth Lort in 1689) or by taking advantage of service to the king to acquire former monastic lands. Over the years most of these families became connected through marriage. Traditionally the Welsh were identified as children of their father. This meant that the sons of Rhys were known as *ap Rhys*, the daughters *ferch Rhys*. Gradually the practice died out and many anglicized the form of the name, so that *ap Rhys* became Price and *ab Owen* became Bowen. (*ab Owen* reflects the use of mutation in the Welsh language whereby a letter changes depending on the word which it precedes or follows, e.g. *bach* meaning little mutates to *fach*, as in *felin fach*).

The Philipps family trace their ancestry to Cadivor Vawr, Lord of Blancych and Cilsant in Carmarthenshire who was one of the earliest Welshmen to side with the Normans. 100 years later, Aaron ap Rhys, Lord of Cilsant travelled to the Holy Land on the crusade with Richard the Lionheart and for his valour in battle at Acre and Arsuf, was awarded the Order of Knighthood of the Sepulchre of our Saviour and the coat of arms of a lion rampant on a field of argent. To this was added a crown and a chain, signifying the family's loyalty to the crown. In the 15th century the head of the family was Fylib ab Ieuan and his grandchildren adopted the anglicized surname of Philipps though with different spellings, Philip ap Philipps Lord of Cilsant and Hugh Phillips of Shropshire. Philip's son Thomas served Henry VIII and fought at the Battle of Tournai. He was knighted and married Joan Dwnn, the heiress of Picton Castle. The Philipps family have been in possession of Picton ever since.

The nature of many villages has changed over the years. Many have disappeared with the reduction of agricultural employment and the demise of many large estates, while others have expanded as commuting centres, through tourism or retirement. Both population and cultural change has seen the closure and sometimes the abandonment of churches and chapels, while the village pub and shop have come under pressure. Such changes are not new; many churches had fallen into a dilapidated state in the 18th and early 19th century before rebuilding in the Victorian era. Non conformity led to the building of large numbers of chapels while the temperance movement saw the closure of many public houses.

Agriculture practices in the county were deemed poor, with the type of plough used in the 19th century reported as having the effectiveness of "a herd of swine moiling it". Carts were drawn by "two oxen yoked abreast, with a long pole to answer the purpose of a shaft, preceded by a pair of horses also abreast". (*The Beauties of England and Wales, or, Delineations, topographical, historical, and descriptive, of each county*, Volume 18, Pub. 1815)

South Pembrokeshire had a thriving coal industry in the 18th and 19th centuries and there was a small iron industry around Saundersfoot. Elsewhere there were large numbers of corn and woollen mills; few of which remain active. Defence has been a major aspect in Pembrokeshire life throughout its history. Iron Age forts, Viking promontory forts, Norman and Welsh castles, 19th century forts around Milford Haven, the training ranges of the two world wars and the airship stations of World War I and airfields of World War II all have left their mark on the county, while the ranges at Castlemartin and Manorbier continue to provide employment.

Milford Haven has played an important role in the history and industry of the county and this role continues with giant oil and gas terminals served by some the world's largest tankers. Pembroke and Fishguard continue as ferry ports as historic links with Ireland continue.

Myths and legends abound in the county. It was claimed that Milford Haven folk could see green fairy islands lying offshore and that the fairies would visit the markets around the Haven sometimes unseen, but would pay the exact money for their purchases without asking the price. It was said that "the Methodists drove away the fairies". Others claim that it was the abstinence from alcohol that accompanied the non-conformist movement that was the cause of their demise. Shakespeare sets his play *Cymbeline*, about the legends of the British King Cubolinus, in Pembrokeshire around the shores of Milford Haven. While there are stories of fairies and ghosts, witchcraft was virtually unknown in Wales

Pembrokeshire has relatively few towns, none large: Haverfordwest, Milford Haven, Narberth, Neyland, Pembroke, Pembroke Dock, Tenby, Newport and Fishguard and Goodwick and Britain's smallest city, St David's. It is in the villages that the bulk of the population live and where the true character of the county is found.

This book aims to give a brief impression of each village and give information on points of interest, history, myths and legends.

Villages of Pembrokeshire

Abercastle

Abercastle is a picturesque little harbour village on the north-west coast seven miles south-west of Fishguard. Today the harbour which is protected by the island of Ynys y Castell, accessible at low tide, is used by pleasure boats, though there is sand at low tide. The remains of store houses are in the village as is the former mill, complete with millstone in the garden, now offering holiday accommodation.

Trade was recorded as far back as the 16th century and continued until the 1920s. Sloops based at Abercastle took corn and butter to Bristol and Liverpool, returning with general merchandise. Smaller vessels brought in coal, culm and limestone from Milford Haven. The remains of a limekiln still stand on the harbour.

Above the village, to the south-west and accessible from the harbour by the Pembrokeshire Coastal Path, is Carreg Samson, a 5000 year old cromlech. Originally covered by earth, the massive capstone, measuring 15ft by 9ft, is supported by just three of the six standing stones. Legend has it that St Samson, a 6th century Celtic Saint with links to Brittany, flicked the capstone from the harbour with his little finger. The cromlech stands in a field belonging to Long House Farm, previously a grange, adjoining and belonging to the Episcopal manor of Trefine, part of the St David's monastic estate.

In 1876 Alfred Johnson landed at Abercastle after making the first solo Atlantic crossing by boat.

Abercych

Abercych is situated in the north-east of the county one and a half miles south-west of Cenarth. The Afon Cych marks the boundary between Pembrokeshire and Carmarthenshire. Abercych is a small ribbon development built on the western side of the valley with the Cych flowing into the Teifi.

There was a corn mill in the village which has been converted into a holiday cottage, though it retains its water wheel and the grindstone forms part of the garden.

The village has two inns, both at the southern end of the village in the area known as Penrhiw. The Nag's Head lies to the south near Pont Treseli, and its beer garden overlooks the Afon Cych. Its sign is believed to be the only one in the world with a biblical quotation "be cunning as a serpent, but peaceful as a dove."*Mathew* 10.16. The inn, a restored smithy, brews its own beer. The Penrhiw Inn is a smaller pub, in premises that were formerly the post office. The new post office is more central to the village, next to Yr Hen Ysgol (the Old School). The village is in the parish of Manordeifi and did have a mission church, dedicated to St John, built using corrugated iron. The site was converted into a community garden in 1999, but has been sadly neglected. Ramoth Baptist Chapel dates from 1826.

The village was celebrated as a centre for the wood turning industry with generations of the Davies family combining farming and wood turning. The valley is well suited to this craft with the woods well stocked with sycamore, the ideal wood for turning. In the 1920s a water driven plant was established by James Davies in the old corn mill in the village. The company, James Davies (Abercych) Ltd, still in the hands of the Davies family, is now located on the River Teifi near Cenarth. The woods of Glyn Cuch are mentioned in the ancient welsh text of the *Mabinogion*.

Abereiddy

Abereiddy is a former slate quarrying centre on the coast of north-west Pembrokeshire, four and a half miles north-east of St David's. There are the remains of quarrymen's cottages and the quarry, which was flooded in a storm and abandoned. The Blue Lagoon is the result of the quarry and is a safe dive site during stormy weather. It was the site for the World Cliff Diving Championships in September 2012, with a 27 metre high diving platform built into the cliff above. A narrow gauge railway took the slate across the headland to Porthgain for shipping. The circular building that stood to the north of the beach was the quarry powder store.

There is a sizeable car park and a good beach with unusually dark sand at low tide.

The headland to the north of the bay is known as Trwyncastell (Castle Point) and has a watchtower but older defensive ramparts and ditches. It is a popular promontory for rock climbing.

The few houses in the hamlet are well protected, with mortared roofs, against the Atlantic gales which are too strong for the soft local slate.

Abereiddy doubled as a Cornish cove in the 1961 film *Fury at Smugglers'Bay*.

Abermawr

There is no village of Abermawr, but a beautiful, sandy, quiet beach except at high tide when there are just pebbles. It is accessible by road from Mathry which lies a mile and a half to the south, but difficult to find. It might however have been very different as Brunel proposed that Abermawr rather than Fishguard should be the ferry terminal for his South Wales Railway. Abermawr was also a cable station, with the first cable to Wexford in Ireland laid in 1862 with further cables enabling links to America. There was a relay station above the beach to forward messages to and from London. The station was abandoned in the 1920s.

It is said that the shingle was deposited after the Royal Charter Storm of 1859 which damaged the nearby church at Cwm yr Eglwys.

The road runs along a wooded valley with Great Mill the only property. There are the remains of the old mill wheel. Half a mile from the beach is Melin Tregwynt, an operating woollen mill that has been in the same family since 1912 and currently employs some 20 people.

Nearby but more difficult to access is Aberbach beach.

Ambleston

Ambleston is a small, pretty village eight miles north of Haverfordwest. The name is derived from Amlot's Farm, though another attribution is to Hamill, a Viking leader. The small Church of St Mary is at the centre of the village and has a Norman squat tower but the rest has been rebuilt. The Norman font was actually sold in 1903 but subsequently returned to the church. At one time the tower had a spire added but this was removed during renovations. The church was granted to the Knights of St John of Jerusalem in the 13th century by the heirs of Wizo of Wiston.

Bethel Calvinistic Methodist Chapel was built in 1881 with further alterations in 1906.

The village has a good mix of old and modern housing with no major developments. It was on the Via Flandrica or Fordd Fleming, which can still be traced from Roch Castle to Ambleston and would have been used by pilgrims en route for St David's. It is thought that the Via Flandrica was an ancient British road, rather than Roman.

Amroth

Amroth today is a seaside village with its sandy beach and the usual array of pubs and ice cream shops two and a half miles north-east of

Saundersfoot. The name is thought to comprise of *am*, about and *rath*, a mound. The population is swelled in the summer months with holiday makers in self-catering accommodation and the many caravans to the west of the village around Amroth Castle. In the 18th and early 19th century however the parish was known for its fine coal and iron ore. There was a small scale iron foundry and coal was exported via the harbour at Wiseman's Bridge to Bristol.

The grounds of Amroth Castle are now used as a park for holiday caravans, with a swimming pool, while the Castle is used as a bar and social club on the ground floor with self-catering accommodation on the upper floor. The present mansion dates from 1800 and was built by Captain James Acland. Prior to this the house was known as Earwear and was in the Eliot family for four and a half centuries. The first Eliot was David Eliot who was steward to the widowed Countess of Pembroke in 1347. The family name changed to the more usual Elliot in the 16th century. The only remnant of the pre-1800 building is the much restored gateway. A castle existed in Amroth prior to the Normans but it stood on higher ground, near the church. Acland had purchased Amroth Castle in 1757 and Nelson stayed here en route to Milford Haven where the Hamiltons were staying. In the 1820s the castle was sold to the Revd Thomas Shrapnel Biddulph, Prebendary of Brecon Cathedral and a relative of the Elliots. In the 1850s it was in use as a lunatic asylum, as evidenced by a letter to *The Times* of 22nd September, 1853 alleging ill treatment of the inmates. It subsequently returned to being a private home and was owned in the early part of the 20th century by Sir Owen Cosby-Philipps.

Cosby-Philipps was a shipping magnate. Starting with one ship in 1888 he eventually owned or controlled a number of shipping lines including the Royal Mail Steam Packet Company, the Union-Castle Line and the Pacific Steam Navigation Company, culminating in the purchase of the White Star Line in 1927. He was at various times MP for Pembroke and Haverfordwest and for Chester. He was made First Baron Kylsant in 1923. Known as an autocrat, in 1931 he was charged with making false statements with regard to his companies'accounts for 1926 and 1927, contrary to Section 84 of the Larceny Act 1861. He was sentenced to a year in prison which he spent in Wormwood Scrubs where he was allowed to have outside caterers supply his food. He lost all his honours. Cosby-Philipps had purchased Plas Llanstephan in Carmarthenshire in 1920 and Amroth Castle was occupied by his daughter the Hon. Mrs Coventry, who had married the heir to the Earl of Coventry. They lived at the Castle until her husband inherited the title in 1930.

The Union Castle ship *Arundel Castle* was originally to have been named Amroth Castle when laid down in 1915.

The church of St Elidyr, with its battlemented tower is situated above the modern village. It was built in 1490 by John Eliot of Earwear to replace two earlier churches and is not on a traditional Celtic llan. In the 16th century John Elliot of Earwear added a chantry chapel which was given to the church by the Biddulphs in the 1890s. Three small bells manufactured in the local foundry were hung in 1712 but these were sent to the Whitechapel Foundry in 1929 to be made into a single bell which was hung in the tower. The remains of a 9th century preaching cross can be found in the church, south of the nave. The dedication to St Elidyr is difficult. It is popular in the area and may relate to Sir Elidur de Stackpole, cross bearer on Archbishop Baldwin's journey through Wales recruiting for the Third Crusade in 1188. Another suggestion is Elidyr the Courteous but this seems unlikely as he was a 6th century prince of Strathclyde, slain in North Wales. A further suggestion is that is a corruption of Eluid, an alternative name for St Teilo.

Angle

Angle is a village on a peninsular at the southern entrance to Milford Haven, eight miles west of Pembroke. The coast is rocky with the exception of West Angle Bay which has a sandy beach with the mud and sand at the sheltered eastern bay used by small boat owners. The village boasts two pubs, the Hibernia in the centre and The Old Point House to the east overlooking the Haven. St Mary's Church in the centre of the village dates from the 14th century with the tower added around 1500, with Victorian refurbishment. In 1175-76 the rector was Giraldus Cambrensis the Welsh historian, a grandson of Gerald of Pembroke and the Welsh native Princess Nest. In the churchyard stands St Anthony's Chapel, a seaman's chapel built in the 15th century, by Edward de Shirburn, to house the bodies of sailors washed up around the coast.

To the north of the village is the lifeboat station established in 1868. The crew were involved in the rescue of the *Loch Shiel* on 30th January, 1894. The ship en route from Glasgow to Adelaide was forced to seek shelter in the Haven but was wrecked on a reef near Thorn Island. The *Loch Shiel* was a sailing ship carrying whisky, much of which was never recovered, at least by the Customs. The wreck lies north of Rat Island.

Tower at Castle Farm

The village has a number of attractive older cottages and houses and the most recent building has been in keeping, though this cannot be said of all the modern housing in the village.

The coast was strategically important and there were three forts around the peninsular guarding the entrance to the Haven. Thorn Island Fort off West Angle Bay was built in the 1850s. It was used as a small hotel from 1932 and was put up for sale in 2011 after being empty for some ten years. Accessible only by sea it has planning permission for a cable car. Chapel Bay Fort, to the north of the village, was a gun battery built in 1891 and another battery was established to the west. South of West Angle Bay is the East Blockhouse. This was one of a pair of forts established in the time of Henry VIII to guard the entrance of the Haven. There are a number of prehistoric forts around the coast signifying the importance of this area over thousands of years.

During World War II an airfield was built south of the village and was the site of the first ground landing of a Sunderland. It was a bomber base for raids on north-west France.

There is a tower in the grounds of Castle Farm thought to have been a medieval moated house, a tidal inlet is nearby. Some 30ft high, consisting of three stories, it may have been the home of Edward de Shirburn, builder of the seamen's chapel nearby. Some have suggested that it was a Pele Tower, but these are restricted to the North-east of England. Some 50 yards away are the remains of a dovecote, a sign of a wealthy house.

The remains of a possible castle are to the south of the main street, opposite the school. The walls are over three feet thick and while it has been described as a castle on old Ordnance Survey maps, it may have been an almshouse or nunnery.

South-east of the village is a Neolithic burial chamber known as the Devil's Quoit., with a capstone measuring 12ft by 8ft.

In the main street stands what was once the Globe Hotel with its crenellated walls. Converted from two cottages in 1904, its colonnade covers the street pavement.

At the eastern end of the village lies Angle Hall, the home since 1800 of the Mirehouse family. Benjamin Heath Malkin in *The Scenery, Antiquities and Biography of South Wales* asserts that "Mr Mirehouse is esteemed to be one of the finest gentleman farmers in the kingdom". In 1800 he was awarded the gold medal for improving waste moors by the Society for the Encouragement of Arts Manufactures and Commerce.

The strip field system still in use to the north of the village dates back to Norman times. Bangeston, the mansion built by the de Beneger family to the south-east of the village, was in ruins by the early 19th century. It was at one time home to Lord Lyon, King of Arms and locals told of "quare doings" at the house at that time. According to local legend, Lord Lyon, one dirty night, drove a coach and horses over a cliff at Freshwater and was never seen again. The Lord Lyon was John Hooke-Campbell whose title was as head of the Scottish equivalent of the College of Arms, a position he held from 1754 to 1796. He was a grandson of Sir Alexander Campbell, the owner of Stackpole through marriage to Elizabeth Lort. There is a problem with the story of the Lord Lyon's disappearance, however, in that he is recorded as dying in Bath. His grandson, Matthew Campbell inherited Bangeston but appears to have had money troubles and stripped the house of its lead and possessions.

Bayvil

Bayvil is an area in north Pembrokeshire, just over a mile north-east of Nevern, the only evidence for which on the map is Bayvil Farm. The church of St Andrew the Apostle is now in the hands of Friends of Friendless Churches and situated near the farm. Dating from medieval times the single cell church was rebuilt early in the 19th century with Georgian features. It has a double bellcote, box pews and a triple decker pulpit. The stream which flows past the church joins the Afon Gamman before joinng the Afon Nyfer near Nevern. The name, it is believed, derives from the Norman Beauvil or Beautiful Place.

Begelly

Begelly is a former mining village five miles from Narberth on the road to Tenby. Coal mining was on a small scale and ceased in the 19th century. The village today is a ribbon development with much new building. There are some attractive older houses and cottages near the church.

The church of St Mary is Norman in origin and has a weeping chancel (the chancel is out of line with the nave representing the leaning of Christ's head at the crucifixion). The embattled tower is Pembrokeshire's tallest church tower at 71 feet and the chancel arch is in the Norman style. There was a restoration in the 1880s when the lych gate was added.

Begelly Hall, near the church is a four storey building, built by local coal owners, the Child family, in the late 18th century. It is now the home of Neil Machin, an artist in wood and courses are offered in woodcarving. The artist Augustus John spent part of his childhood in the 'Big House' in the village.

Zion Methodist Chapel was built in 1828 and rebuilt in 1866. Together with the school and schoolhouse it is Grade II listed.

The Welsh spelling is Begeli and means Bugail's Land.

To the north of Begelly is Folly Farm, a farm based theme park and Zoo. It also houses a large undercover funfair.

Berry Hill

Berry Hill is north-east of Newport on the coast road. Berry Hill House is one of the largest farmhouses in the county dating from the 18th-19th century. The farm is still active, but there are no other properties. According to Samuel Lewis in his *Topographical Dictionary of Wales* of 1833, the name of the house was Burry, the residence of the female branch of the Bowens; Fenton refers to it as Bury. To the east of Berry Hill is Llwyngwair, now a hotel and caravan park. The hotel building has parts dating back to the 13th century with an 18th century façade. It was the home of the Bowen family from the 16th century until 1956 and was visited by John Wesley, a family friend, who used it as a base for his trips to Ireland. George Bowen (1722-1810) had raised the troops which defeated the French in their invasion of 1797, he was by all accounts a good landlord and was the first in the area to use marl to enrich the soil. He apparently had a machine to mix seaweed, crushed bones and marl which was then used as a fertilizer.

The Bowens were one of the oldest Pembrokeshire families, with marriage links to the other gentry of the county, including the Philipps of Picton Castle. This did not prevent quarrels arising and on 16th June, 1578, John Johnes of Trecwn was murdered at Newport fair by Griffith Philipps of Penypark, aided by James Bowen of Llwyngwair.

Blackpool Mill (See Bluestone)

Blaenffos

A ribbon development on the A478 Tenby to Cardigan road a little under six miles from Cardigan, Blaenffos has a range of older and modern properties. Set in open countryside, the village has the recently refurbished Baptist Chapel and a village store, but no church or pub. The chapel was one of the earliest in Pembrokeshire and was rebuilt in 1856. The village lost its school in 2004. The name means the source of a ditch.

Bletherston

Bletherston is a small community deep in the countryside six miles north-west of Narberth. The little church of St Mary is medieval in origin with alterations and the South Aisle added in the 16th century. It was refurbished in 1886. There is a bellcote but no tower. It is thought that the original Celtic church was dedicated to St Elen otherwise spelt Helen, Welsh wife of the Roman Emperor Magnus Maximus. The Welsh name of the village is Tref Elen and there is an Elen's Well in the nearby parish of Llawhaden, of which Bletherston was a chapelry. Helen is mentioned in the *Mabinogion* in "The Dream of Maxen the Gwledig". Maximumus was Emperor 383 to 388. He was a Spaniard who was in command of the Roman legions in Britain and became Emperor of the Western Empire with his capital centred on Triers, the Roman Augusta Treverorum. His wife is said to have given her palace to the church and it became Triers Cathedral. The death of Maximus saw the end of Roman rule in the north of the Empire, including Britain. According to legend Helen was a prolific road builder, hence the Roman road known as Sarn Helen.

Bluestone

Bluestone is a holiday complex built in the form of a village with 335 timber lodges. Taking its name from the Pembrokeshire Bluestones that form part of Stonehenge, it occupies part of what was Newton North, a small parish two and a half miles south-west of Narberth. The church dating from the 12th century was a roofless ruin by 1900 and its dedication is unknown. The ruins are now a central feature of the Holiday Village and as such the ruins will be preserved. Next to the church is a holy well.

Nearby is the site of Castell Coch, which itself was replaced by the now demolished Newhouse Mansion with its site and gardens now mingled with the site of the castle.

Within the old parish of Newton North is Blackpool Mill, a four storey corn mill built in 1813, recently restored and open to the public. The tide mill turbine is still operational.

1080 yards east of the entrance is the ruined Mounton Chapel, a ruin now threatened by encroaching vegetation. Although a public footpath passes the church, where the structure of nave, chancel and bellcote is still visible, access is prevented by a fence and 'Keep Out' notices.

Boncath

Boncath is a 19th century railway village in north Pembrokeshire, five miles from Newcastle Emlyn. The name is derived from the Welsh for Buzzard. Only one cottage was present in 1840. The parish church is now the former Cilwendeg Estate church of St Colman, built in the 1830s. The design is unusual with its whitewashed walls and tower and is to be found down Capel Colman Lane east of the village. St Colman was an Irish Saint.

The church of St Michael at Penbedw Farm, to the north, is medieval in origin but is now in a sad state of decay, being used to house Shetland ponies.

The village has an inn on the crossroads, the Boncath Inn, but little of interest in the village itself which is a mixture of 19th and 20th century buildings.

Cilwendeg Mansion was built in the 1780s by Morgan Jones and it is one of Pembrokeshire's most important mansions. It was acquired by the County Council in 1952 and used as a care home but was put on the market in 2010. The mansion and a number of other buildings on the estate are listed. Most noteworthy is the Pigeon House built in 1835 to house dogs, ducks, turkeys and geese on the ground floor, hens on the first floor and pigeons on the upper shelves.

Bosherston

Bosherston is five and a half miles south of Pembroke. Originally known as Stackpole Bosher having been granted to a servant of the de Stackpole family, it became known as Bosher's Town and then Bosherston. It is thought that the Stackpoles arrived with William the Conqueror and adopted the name in referring to Stack Pool near the Stack Rock.

Bosherston is an attractive village apart from some out of character mid-20th century development and is close to a number of local attractions. A number of the houses date from the 18th century. Look out for the large square chimneys local to Pembrokeshire.

The church of St Michael and All Angels dates from the 13th century and is a cruciform shape. The font is Norman but the 1855 restoration, funded by Lord Cawdor, installed neo Gothic windows, replacing the Norman. Outside the church is a preaching cross with a face carving said to represent Christ. The chancel has a plain double piscina and an aumbry originally used for storing chalices and the reserved sacrament, while in the south-west angle is a squint. There are two tombs with effigies attributed by *Archaelogia Cambrensis* 1909 to the 14th century. Guide books identify one as probably the Dowager Duchess of Buckingham, an antecedent of the Duke of Norfolk, though why the Dowager Duchess would be buried here is something of a mystery, especially as the title only came into existence in the 15th century. The other is of a crusader. In the 15th century it was referred to as the church of Stackpole Bosher.

In the village there is the St Govan's Inn and 'Ye Olde Worlde Café'. St Govan was a 6th century holy man who lived in a cave in the cliffs. The identity of the saint is uncertain, and a number of legends surround him and his identity. In some stories he was Sir Gawain of Arthurian legend, others portray him as an Irishman seeking his former tutor or as a reformed thief. He was set upon by pirates and the rock opened up to present a cave large enough for him to hide. Another story is that as he was fleeing, farmers were ploughing a field and he asked them to tell any pursuers that asked that they had seen him as they were ploughing. By a miracle, three days later the corn was ripe and they were harvesting when the pursuers arrived and the farmers duly answered as the saint had instructed, so the pursuers gave up their search. A further legend is that pirates stole his bell, but angels retrieved it and protected it by covering it in stone and leaving it at the foot of the cliff as Bell Rock.

A 13th to 14th century chapel dedicated to St Govan stands concealed amid the cliffs a mile south of the village. A road leads to a car park from where steps lead down to the little chapel, measuring just 18 by 12 feet. It was a site of pilgrimage in medieval times and the nearby well was held to have miraculous properties, particularly in respect of lameness and eyesight. The bellcote is empty, no doubt the source of the story of Bell Rock.

St Govan's Head is the most southerly point in the county. It forms part of the Castlemartin Artillery Range and may be off-limits at certain times. When Mary Morgan visited in 1791, there was an old woman living opposite the chapel who guided visitors and provided them with water from the well. She was given an income by Lord Cawdor on condition that she took no money from visitors. Mrs Morgan also relates that there is a recess in the chapel and anyone who reclines within it is granted whatever they desire. Single young

St Govan's chapel

ladies prayed for husbands and childless wives for children. It is said that it is impossible to count the number of steps down to the chapel as the number coming up differs from the number of steps on the descent.

To the north-west of the chapel is Huntsman's Leap, a narrow gorge cut into the cliffs almost 200 yards long, but at its narrowest just 18ft wide. According to legend, a huntsman succeeded in jumping the gorge only to perish from sheer fright on reaching his home. To the west of Huntsman's leap the sea has created a blowhole which in stormy weather sees the sea spout way above the land. It was said that sheep and cattle were sucked into the blowhole as the waves receded, never to be seen again. Further along is Buckspool Camp, the remains of an Iron Age/ Roman fortification, with an arch created by the sea beneath.

Bosherston was part of the Stackpole estate, the ownership of which came into the hands of the Campbell family through the marriage of Sir Alexander Campbell, 16th Thane of Cawdor (not related to Macbeth) to the Welsh heiress Elizabeth Lort in 1689. Further marriages brought additional wealth and in 1804 John Frederick Campbell inherited the estates of the Earl of Carbery in Carmarthenshire.

The Cawdors lived at Stackpole and to enhance the view dammed one of three valleys. Eventually it was decided to dam the three glacial valleys and the result was the Bosherston Lily Ponds and lakes. Covering 80 acres they form the largest stretch of fresh water in the Pembrokeshire Coast National Park and are part of the Stackpole National Nature Reserve. The Lily Ponds are found just east of the village and while at their best when the lilies are in full bloom, form attractive walks year round. They are a haven for wildlife with swans, cormorants, kingfishers, buzzards and more than twenty species of duck.

At the end of the lake is Broad Haven, a beautiful sandy beach. It is accessible either from the walk past the Lily Ponds or from the car park signposted at Bosherston.

Two and a half miles west of Bosherston, in the heart of the Castlemartin range is Flimston Chapel. Dating from the 5th century it was restored in 1903 by the Lambton family of Brownslade as a memorial to their sons killed in the Boer War. It was restored again in 1970 by the occupants of the camp. This simple chapel with its bellcote, vestry and porch can be accessed at certain times and the key can be obtained from the Castlemartin guardroom.

Boulston

Named after the Norman, Adam le Bull, Boulston occupies a promontory on a bend in the Western Cleddau, three miles south of Haverfordwest. The Boulston estate came into the hands of the Wogan family by the marriage of Henry Wogan of Milton, son of Sir John Wogan of Wiston, to Margaret Dyer of Boulston. In the late 18th century the estate passed into the hands of the Ackroyd family. Boulston Manor was built in 1798 and is available for bed and breakfast or self-catering. To the south-east of the manor are the remains of the original Elizabethan house which was in ruins in 1811. Remnants of the formal Elizathen walled garden with its terrace overlooking the estuary remain as does the fish pond.

Legend has it that the woods were the home of a basilisk, a reptile that could kill with a single look, but if seen first would itself die. The creature was tricked by a man hiding in a barrel and died. The Wogan family crest of a wyvern is thought to have resulted from this legend.

The parish church now in ruins lies at the water's edge surrounded by trees. Originally a private mausoleum for the Wogan family, it was rebuilt in 1843 by Robert Innes Ackland but has now sadly fallen into ruin. Various monuments from the church are now held at Uzmaston church.

Brawdy

Brawdy is now a district rather than a village and is known as the site of a Royal Air Force and Fleet Air Arm base. Established in World War II, it was handed to the Fleet Air Arm, in 1946, who left in 1971. It was taken over by the RAF between 1974 and 1992 and is now the home of the electronic warfare arm of the Royal Signals.

The name Brawdy is an anglicized form of the Welsh name for Bridget. Situated on the north-east corner of St Bride's Bay, Brawdy has a long history. Brawdy House was the old manor house rebuilt in the late 18th century. The farm buildings surrounding the house date from 1740.

The nearby church of St David was built in 1326 and retains much of its 14th century features. There is a bellcote at both ends of the nave. The church has three early Christian stones, two with Ogham script which are damaged and incomplete.

To the east of Brawdy Farm is Brawdy Castle, an Iron Age, Romano British fort above the confluence of two streams. To the south and east there is a natural escarpment while protection from the north and west is provided by three banks and ditches still clearly defined beneath the wooded hill.

To the north of the airfield is Rickstone Hall, an 18th century farmhouse built from the dismantled earlier manor. The gardens, farm buildings, carriage house and privy are all listed buildings.

To the west, just off the A487 is the motte of Pointz or Punch Castle, a 12th century structure built by Punch, a tenant of the Bishop of St David's.

Bridell

Set in an undulating landscape four miles south of Cardigan on the A478, Bridell is a small village. The parish church of St David is just off the main road, "beautifully situated and embosomed among trees". Originally a chapel of Manordeifi, the church is on an ancient site but dates from the 14th century. It has a single nave with a bellcote and buttressed west wall. Malkin in 1803 described the church interior as clean, "though in point of architecture, little better than a barn".

In the churchyard is a 5th or 6th century seven foot high stone with Ogham script translated as 'Nettasagni son of the descendant of Brecos'. The small carved Celtic cross is believed to be a later 9th century addition.

Plas y Bridell was a Carmelite Convent. The present building dates from 1882 and is now a nursing home.

Broad Haven

Broad Haven is the largest beach resort on Pembrokeshire's west coast. It has a stretch of nearly three quarters of a mile of sandy beach at low tide. There has been a large amount of modern development, swamping the few older properties in the village. The sea front has the usual mix of pubs, takeaways and beach shops, mixed with holiday apartments and a caravan park at the northern end of the beach.

Broadmoor

Broadmoor is a village on the B4586 and straddling the A477 two and a half miles north-west of Saundersfoot. A ribbon development with a mixture of housing, Broadmoor has four caravan parks, taking advantage of its position within three miles of the coast. On the junction with the A477 is the Cross Inn.

While Broadmoor takes advantage of the holiday trade today, it originated as a mining village in the early 19th century, continuing until 1926. There is a row of cottages built for miners by the owners of the Greenhill Colliery, which operated between 1853 and 1881.

Broadway

Broadway is a small hamlet in open countryside on the A4341 road to Broad Haven. Centred on Broadway Farm, just off the main road is the delightfully named Creampots caravan and camping site.

Brynberian

Just off the B4329, three and a quarter miles south-west of Eglwyswrw, is the hamlet of Brynberian. The name is thought to mean the 'Hill of the Kite', from the Welsh for the red kite, *beri*. There is a Welsh Independent chapel which was founded in 1690, one of the earliest in the area. It was rebuilt in 1808 and again in 1843 with renovations in 1882, 1907 and 1961. In the wooded valley is an early 19th century corn mill, Felin Bryn, just above the weir. The hamlet grew around the chapel and also the woollen factory which was in use in the early to mid 19th century. There was some small scale development along the main road during the 19th century. The Afon Brynberian flows from Mynydd Preseli. The moorland on the southern side of the B4329 has a number of Neolithic monuments including Bedd yr Afanc, a chambered long cairn containing a gallery grave.

Brynberian Bridge dates from 1600.

Bryn Henllan (Old Church Hill)

Bryn Henllan sits at the base of Dinas Island, between the bays of Cwm yr Eglwys and Pwllgwaelod. It is an attractive village with a mixture of housing styles. The church of St Brynach was built to replace the destroyed church at Cwm yr Eglwys, which was the Dinas parish church. The church has an unusual offset gabled porch with the door facing east and a low squat belfry with slated roof.

The Calvinistic Methodist chapel in the village is of particular note for its interior which has a gallery supported by marbled wooden columns, though sadly broken windows and an entrance overgrown with weeds tell a sad story.

There is no public house in the village though there is the Old Sailor at Pwllgwaelod and the Freemasons Hotel at Dinas Cross.

Burton

Burton is an attractive village set above the north bank of the Cleddau east of Neyland. There is a good mix of housing and The Stable Inn. The church of St Mary is to be found on Church Lane. An interesting church dating from the 14th century, though much restored in 1865. There are

monuments in the church to members of a number of leading
Pembrokeshire families including the Philipps and Wogans. The organ loft
is an unusual semicircular structure. Outside the church, set against
the south-west wall, is a large restored holy well once used as a baptistery,
and the medieval base of a cross with a 19th century upper section.

A lane leads from Church Lane to Rudders Boatyard and moorings.
The name Burton is thought to be a Saxon variation of the word Briton,
or derived from the Old English *Burgh-tun*, a fortified dwelling place.

Burton Ferry

Burton Ferry is on the north shore of the Daugleddau (Two Cleddau
Rivers) opposite Pembroke Dock and was the ferry terminal for the
river crossing before the opening of the Cleddau Bridge. Most of the
housing is modern, taking advantage of the superb views across the
tidal river and the bridge. The Jolly Sailor is a popular pub and there
are jetties and a slipway.

A hard was constructed in 1942 in preparation for Operation
Overlord, the 1944 invasion of France. It was one of a large number of
such structures around the coasts of South Wales and England to
allow the rapid embarkation of large numbers of troops and
equipment. It was in use until December 1944. It is situated 600 yards
to the east of the Jolly Sailor, just beyond the later NATO Quay.

Bwlch y Groes

Bwlch y Groes is a small hamlet on a crossroads, five miles south-west
of Newcastle Emlyn. In the heart of agricultural countryside, there is
the 1777 Calvinistic Methodist Chapel, a farm foods store and garage.
There has been limited modern development of a few bungalows. The
name means 'Pass of the Cross'.

Caerfarchell

Caerfarchell is a pretty hamlet with no modern developments three
miles east of St David's, south of the A487. A Calvinistic Methodist
Chapel was established in 1737 although the first chapel building was
in 1763. The present chapel was built in 1827 but the upstairs seating
is thought to have been reused from the 17th century building which
occupied the site of the 1928 school. Local legend has it that a horse's
head was incorporated in each of the four corners in the belief that
this would stop echoes, which had been a problem in the earlier chapel.

There is a village green and, at the north-west end, a studio pottery.

Camp Hill

A hamlet on the A478 south of Narberth, Camp Hill has two holiday caravan parks, some old cottages and new bungalows and houses. There is a small tool hire depot and a sand and gravel merchant occupying the quarry site which is now disused.

There is an Iron Age defended enclosure on the hillside overlooking Narberth with the strongest defences on the top of the hill.

Camrose

Camrose is a delightful village, deep in the Pembrokeshire countryside north-west of Haverfordwest. The name is derived from the Welsh Camros or Crooked Moor. The church of St Ismael is 13th century in origin with the tower added in the 15th century and renovations in 1850, 1883 and 2001. The body of the church is unusually long, while the tower stairs form a separate structure to the tower itself. The bellcote is between the nave and chancel, forming a Sanctus bell.

The pretty little Lebanon Baptist Chapel was built in 1838 and rebuilt in 1876.

Across the Camrose Brook to the south of the village is the former water mill, now converted for holiday accommodation, as is the nearby Camrose House. In the garden of the house is a 19th century viewing platform, the remnant of the motte of Camrose Castle. William the Conqueror stayed here on his pilgrimage to St David's in 1081. The house was the seat of the Bowen family after John ab Owen married Jane Roblyn, a descendant of Sir William Roblyn. Owen (Anglicized to Bowen) was a descendant of Bleddyn, the 11th century Prince of Powys. In the 17th century Morgan Bowen, the then head of the family, was accused of murdering a local man by hitting him over the head with a stick, he also attacked his father with a sword and his wife with sheaf picks. (Source Jon Hudson)

Capel Newydd

Capel Newydd or New Chapel is a village on the B4332 a mile and a half north-east of Boncath. A ribbon development with a mixture of housing, Capel Newydd formed around the Calvinistic Methodist chapel built in 1763 and rebuilt in 1848. The building which has a long wall entry is Grade II listed on account of its 1848 interior. The Ffynnone Arms is named after the Ffynnonau Mansion, a mile south-east of the village. The mansion was designed by John Nash and built for John Colby in 1795. It was subsequently extended with a Doric portico in 1830 and new wings in 1904. The building is listed as one of Nash's early works and as one of the finest Edwardian buildings in Wales.

Carew

Carew is a village east of Pembroke Dock dominated by its castle, built to guard a crossing of the Carew River, which at one time was navigable to this point. The name derives from the Welsh Caer Rhiw, meaning Fort on a Low Hill. There is evidence of a castle on this site from the Iron Age and it may have been still in use when the Normans built their first motte and bailey castle here in 1100. The Norman builder was Gerald of Windsor, later to be known as Gerald of Pembroke. He became the owner of the castle and land at Carew as part of the dowry of his wife, the Princess Nest, daughter of Rhys ap Tewdor, the last King of Deheubarth (roughly equivalent to Carmarthenshire, Pembrokeshire and Cardiganshire) who was killed at the Battle of Brecon in 1093. The eldest son of Gerald de Windsor and the Princess Nest adopted the name de Carew. Gerald's castle

Carew castle

was of timber and while later, in the 12th century, the Old Tower had been built to protect the entrance, the main structure was built by the Carew family in stages before Sir Edward de Carew leased the estate to Rhys ap Thomas, the leader of the Welsh in the late 1480s. Rhys had gained great wealth from his support of Henry Tudor and legend has it that he struck the blow that killed Richard III at the Battle of Bosworth. Rhys set about converting the castle into the palatial home of a wealthy Tudor gentleman, complete with a deer park. According to Leland, Rhys held a Tournament for Henry Tudor lasting five days before the Battle of Bosworth. It was a "festivall and time of jollite" and "tentes and pavilions were pitched in the parke neere to the castle". However it is believed that Rhys held the tournament on St George's Day, 1507 following his admission to the Order of the Garter. Rhys had one legitimate son and 14 illegitimate children who all married well. Rhys's grandson however fell foul of Henry VIII and was executed for treason and his estates passed to the Crown. Eventually, Rhys's descendants regained much of their estates and became Barons of Dynevor in Carmarthenshire, the seat of their ancestor, the Lord Rhys.

The castle was passed to Sir John Perrot in 1558 and it was he who built the north wing, the last addition to the castle. After Sir John's death in 1592, while awaiting his sentence for treason, an inventory revealed that there were 58 feather beds, 14 tables but only 15 chairs at Carew. There were 95 horses, 400 head of cattle and 1500 sheep. At the time of the succession of Charles I Carew was owned by the crown and the tenant was Sir John Carew who persuaded Charles that misfortune met any owner of the estate who was not a descendant of Gerald de Windsor. Charles was convinced and passed ownership to Sir John.

The castle is apparently haunted. There have been sightings of a Celtic warrior on the battlements, a kitchen boy who bangs pots and pans, a white lady floating from room to room and, most intriguingly, a Barbary ape.

In 1644 the castle was taken by the Roundheads under Rowland Laugharne with a skirmish fought in the meadows just south of the village. After the Civil War the Castle gradually fell into ruins.

The Castle is now owned by the Carew family but leased to the Pembrokeshire National Park.

The ruins of Carew Castle are among the most magnificent in South Wales, but the village has more to offer, including the Carew Cross adjacent to the main road. The 11th century Celtic Cross stands some

13 feet high and is a memorial to Maredudd ab Edwin, joint ruler of Deheubarth who died in 1035.

Beyond the Castle is the French Mill and dam, a rare example of a tidal flour mill. The present structure dates from the 18th century, but the original mill was much earlier, with references to it as far back as 1476. The building is now a museum but the two undershot water wheels which powered seven millstones are still in place.

In Bird's Lane is a chimney dating from the 15th-16th century with two ovens. The terrace of cottages in Bird's Lane certainly dates from the 18th century, but may be earlier.

The church of St Mary is situated at Carew Cheriton half a mile to the south of the village across the A477. The church dates from the 14th century with nave, aisles and porch added in the 15th century and the tower added in 1500. There is a piscina and sedilia and a curious stone figure supposed to be of a boy bishop elected by his fellow choristers. There are also figures of a monk and a knight in armour with sword, shield and legs crossed. The floor tiles have the emblems of the Bishop of St David's, Sir Rhys ap Thomas and the Tudor Rose.

In the churchyard is the old school house. Described as St

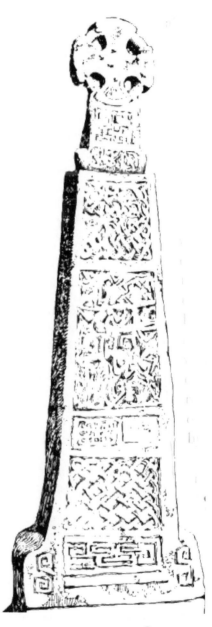

Carew cross

Mary's school in 1625 and used as such until 1872 it is thought to be a 14th century mortuary chapel.

Across the stream from the church is the old fortified rectory. Now a private house, the rectory has a tower thought to date from the 15th or early 16th century. It was garrisoned during the English Civil War.

Carew Newton

Carew Newton is a small hamlet north of Carew. There has been little modern development and there are some attractive old barns and farm buildings. The Cambrian Archaeological Association in 1857 reported several perfect Flemish medieval houses. Aerial photographs reveal that it may have been a much larger village in medieval times. South-east of the hamlet is an active stone quarry.

Zoar Congregational Chapel was built in 1865 and rebuilt in 1912. It has now been converted into a private home.

Carregwen (See Manordeifi)

Carnhedryn

Carnhedryn is a small hamlet on the A487 three and a half miles north-east of St David's. The old school is now a fabric showroom and the Victorian church of St James, which was a chapel of ease to Llanhowell, is now a private dwelling. A 5th–6th century inscribed stone was discovered at Carnhedryn Uchaf Farm, being used as a gatepost. It was installed in the porch of St James church, but is now in the church at Llanhowell. (See Treglemais)

Castlebythe

Castlebythe is a small farming community under Mynydd Castlebythe six miles south-east of Fishguard. There is no new development but some older buildings are being restored. There is what is believed to be a motte in Lower Castlebythe Farm. 300 yards to the east is Castell y Fuwch, the clear remains of an Iron Age fort defined by a bank and ditch with a further rampart to the north. There are signs of buildings having been erected in the enclosure. The name Castell y Fuwch means Cow Castle. Higher up on Mynydd Castlebythe are two ring barrows. At 347 metres above sea level, Mynydd Castlebythe gives superb views across Pembrokeshire and out to sea.

The parish church of St Michael is now in ruins, with walls reduced to a little over three foot. The church, which was 13th century, is in the centre of the community and the graveyard and church are accessible. The last burial was in 1979.

To the west of the farm is Castlebythe Common in which is Fynnon Mihangel, St Michael's Spring.

Castlemartin

Castlemartin is a village in the far south-west of the county with an Iron Age/medieval double banked enclosure in the centre of the village. The 13th century church which is dedicated to St Martin, giving the village its name, is situated to the north on Church Lane. It is a large church with a limestone tower with louvred windows to the bell chamber, standing next to the south porch. There are two aisles separated by graceful arches and a chancel. There is access from the porch to the tower. Behind the church are the ruins of the rectory built in the 12th century.

The area to the south of the village is now an army artillery range with restricted access. For 35 years, from 1961, it was used by the West German as well as the British Army for training. The area has a number of Iron Age forts and round barrows as well as a possible later chapel and burial site. There is a lake and the remains of Frainslake Corn Mill dating from the 16th century. The coast around has a number of arches and sandy bays which are within the danger area and the Pembrokeshire Coastal Path diverts inland between Elegug Stacks and Freshwater West bay. Elegug is an old name for the guillemot, and the Stacks were so named because of the large number of elegugs nesting there.

Entering Castlemartin the traffic roundabout was the 18th century village pound for stray animals. Past the pound there are two semi detached single storey cottages. These were originally three 18th century two roomed 'poor-houses', improved in the 19th century by Lord Cawdor and subsequently modernised. There has been little modern development in the village and a number of houses date from the 18th century.

In the 19th century, the *Penny Cyclopaedia* reported that the breed of Black Cattle known as the Castle Martin breed "were bought in droves for the supply of the London market". Agriccultor writing in *The Farmer's Magazine* in 1834 reported that "in the neighbourhood of Castle Martin I had the opportunity of seeing many specimens of the best breeding in the country"

Mary Morgan in her *Tour to Milford Haven* relates the story that Henry Reynolds of Pennyhold, a farmer of good reputation was standing on the shore near Castlemartin in December 1782 and saw a strange creature in the sea. From a distance of just 10 yards he saw a youth of sixteen, with white skin, sitting in the water in an erect posture with his waist upwards out of the water, which was quite deep at this point. The body appeared to grow from a brown substance under the water and there was a tail which resembled that of a large conger eel which continually moved in a circular fashion. He observed that the body from waist up was human, but with hands and arms appearing short and thick in relation to his body. The head was human too, but the nose rose high between the eyes and from the forehead was a brownish substance, long, three or four fingers wide which went over his head and down the back, but there was no hair. The creature made no noise though it looked wild and fierce. Reynolds observed it for an hour, swimming around a rock, but when he returned with others it had disappeared. The Pennyhold referred to by Mrs Morgan is Pen-y-Holt, now in the Castlemartin Danger Area.

At Furzenip at the southern end of Freshwater West Bay is a restored seaweed drying shelter. Seaweed was gathered for the production of the Welsh delicacy, laverbread. Originally there were four such huts here and the last one was restored with a new thatch roof by volunteers in the 1970s.

The coast around Castlemartin has seen a number of shipwrecks over the years, with burials locally, including: the passengers and crew of the *Edinburgh*, bound from New Orleans to Liverpool, which was wrecked on Linney Head on 8th February, 1839; the owner and members of the crew of the schooner *Wave of Aberystwyth*, wrecked in Freshwater Bay, 26th October, 1859; 21 passengers, officers and crew of the *Mars* en route from Waterford to Bristol, wrecked off Linney Head, 1st April, 1862; members of the crew of *S. S. Tormer*, wrecked off Linney Head, 30th October, 1894; the crew of H.M. Transport *Ionian* wrecked off Linney Head, 20th October, 1917. (These men are commemorated by graves, under the care of the Imperial War Graves Commission.)

Castlemorris

Castlemorris is a quiet village on the B4331 south-west of Fishguard. There is a large agricultural feed supplier on the main road but the major part of the village is to the south with a small village green.

Named after a motte and bailey castle which overlooked the Western Cleddau, there is no sign of the motte and there is no indication of its existence on the Ordnance Survey map. It was mentioned in 1326 in the *Black Book* of St David's.

To the north of the village is Llangloffan Farm which makes cheese and is open for demonstrations of cheese making. There is a Baptist Chapel established in 1706.

One and a quarter miles south-east of Castlemorris is Priskilly House, now part of the Priskilly Forest Country House and Golf Club. The Georgian mansion was the home to a branch of the Harries family. The founder of the family was a Norman and the earliest recorded name was Fromond Brown. The family adopted the Welsh custom of sons taking their father's Christian name and Lewis ap Harry eventually adopted the Harries surname. The original owners were the Owens but in the 17th century John Harries married Letitia Owen and their son George inherited the Priskilly estate.

Cheriton or Stackpole Elidor

Situated on a crossroads at the head of the wooded valley that leads to the Stackpole Lakes, Cheriton consists of a few houses including the Smithy and the church of St James and St Elidyr which dates from the 12th century. The church of the Stackpole estate of the Cawdor family, it was selected as one of Sir John Betjeman's Best British Churches. It was restored in 1851 by the architect Sir George Gilbert Scott. Scott was one of the great architects of the Victorian age and his work included the Albert Memorial, Glasgow University, Bombay University, Christchurch Cathedral New Zealand, the cathedral of St John's Newfoundland, the Foreign Office and the Midland Grand Hotel at St Pancras Station. The tower which contains three bells is the oldest part of the church while Scott retained the 14th century transept vaulting. In the chapel is an inscribed 5th-6th century pillar with Latin text translated as Camulorix, son of Fannucus. The Cawdor coat of arms is a feature of the chancel flooring. The lych-gate is Art Nouveau in style, dating from 1898. There is a tomb chest with the effigies of Sir Elidor de Stackpole and his wife Elspeth. Giraldus Cambrensis tells the story of Sir Elidor's steward, Simon, who seized the keys from the former steward and assumed his duties. He catered for every whim of Sir Elidor, knowing his wishes in advance. The food for masters and servants was of the highest quality, but he never went to church and it was discovered that he held conversations at night near a millpond. Confronted, Simon admitted to being the product of a liaison between his mother and a demon who had assumed the appearance of her dead husband. Simon was dismissed.

On the south side of the church is the small Lort Chapel, named after Roger Lort the 16th century Lord of the Manor of Stackpole. There is an imposing monument to Roger and his wife Abertha, with their seven sons and five daughters depicted at the base. There is also the Tomb of John Campbell, the First Earl Cawdor.

Cilgerran

Cilgerran is an ancient village, formerly a borough. Its long High Street is full of character houses and now has a tranquillity that belies its busy past when it hosted a regular Thursday market and fairs on 22nd August and 12th November. The markets had ceased by the start of the 19th century though the fairs continued for some time. Perched above a gorge of the River Teifi, which forms the northern boundary of the county, Cilgerran is just two miles south of Cardigan town. A former slate quarrying village, Dolbadau Quarries were located to the east.

The name is believed to have been derived from 'Cil', meaning a place of retreat and 'Gerran', from Geraint, son of Erbin, a prince of Devon. Another more fanciful translation is 'Narrow are thy walls'.

Cilgerran is best known for its castle. Standing on a cliff above the confluence of the Afon Plysgog and the River Teifi Cilgerran is one of the most imposing of Welsh Castles and has attracted many artists over the centuries including J.M.W. Turner and the Welsh artist, Richard Wilson, regarded as the father of British landscape art. As well as his painting of Cilgerran in the National Museum of Wales, he incorporated the scene as the backdrop to *The Destruction of Niobe's Children.* Guarding a crossing of the Teifi, which was navigable to this point, the castle was in a key location. It is thought to have been established in the early years of the 12th century by Gerald of Windsor as Cenarth Bychan. It is generally accepted that it was from here that Gerald's wife Nest, known as the Helen of Wales, was abducted by her cousin Owain ap Cadwgan, son of the Prince of Powys. (Other suggestions as the site for the attack and abduction are Pembroke Castle and Carew Castle.)

Nest was the daughter of Rhys ap Tewdur, King of Deheubarth, who was killed in 1093 at the Battle of Brecon. Nest was made a ward of the future Henry I and married to Gerald of Windsor by whom she had three sons and two daughters. Her brother, Gruffydd ap Rhys escaped to Ireland. As part of her dowry Gerald had gained substantial land in Pembrokeshire and was made Constable of Pembroke Castle. The story goes that Owain attacked the castle at night in 1109 and Nest encouraged her husband to escape via the gardrobe (the lavatory outlet). Nest was raped and she and the children were taken to a hunting lodge north of Llangollen. The children were returned to their father and Nest followed shortly afterwards, Owain and his father being forced to seek refuge in Ireland.

Gruffydd returned from Ireland in 1112 and stayed with Gerald and Nest before attempting to regain his inheritance. He married Gwenllian, daughter of the King of Gwynedd and for a number of years fought a guerrilla campaign against the Normans. In an attempt to capture Gruffydd, Gerald led an army north from Pembroke which was to meet a Welsh army under the now pardoned Owain. Gruffydd was nowhere to be found but Gerald took the opportunity to gain revenge on Owain who was killed in the battle.

In addition to her children by Gerald, Nest had a son by Henry I, Henry Fitzroy and following the death of Gerald she married Stephen, Constable of Cardigan Castle.

The Fitzgeralds of Ireland are descended from Gerald and Nest and their grandson Gerald de Barry is better known as the writer and historian Gerald of Wales. His uncle, David Fitzgerald was Bishop of St David's. Their eldest son adopted the surname de Carew.

The first mention of Cilgerran was in 1164, when the castle was taken by the Lord Rhys, son of Nest's brother Gruffydd. He managed to regain his grandfather's kingdom, albeit by paying homage to Henry II. It was recaptured in 1204 by William Marshal, Earl of Pembroke but retaken by Llewellyn the Great in 1215. It was again taken by William Marshal (the son), who was responsible for the building of much of the castle, the remains of which are seen today. It was strengthened in the 1370s but taken by Owain Glyndwr in his revolt of 1405. The castle was badly damaged in this attack and for a short time became a home for the Carmarthenshire Vaughan family under Henry VII.

In the 18th century the ruined castle became a tourist attraction, with visitors coming by boat from Cardigan. It was the setting of a poem *The Grave of King Arthur* by Thomas Warton the Poet Laureate 1785-90, which describes minstrels telling the story of King Arthur at a dinner at Cilgerran before Henry II on the eve of his sailing to Ireland, though the actual dinner took place at Pembroke Castle.

A road from the village runs down to the river where there is a car park and picnic area and a walk, part of the old towpath, through the gorge to Lechryd Bridge. There is a good view of the castle and upstream there are the remains of a quay used for barges to transport materials to and from the Castell Malgwyn tinplate works, situated 150 yards further upstream. The river is still tidal at the quay. The works were established around 1772 when an Act of Parliament allowed the building of a channel from Manordeifi to carry a reliable source of water to the works. Built by the Penygored Company, it was the second largest tinplate works in Britain. It was purchased in 1791 by Sir John Hammet who built Castell Malgwyn House and established the surrounding estate. The works had closed by 1810 and the buildings demolished though remains of the two furnaces are still visible. Castell Malgwyn House is now a hotel, renamed Hammet House.

Cilgerran has three inns, the 17th century Pendre Inn, the tiny Masons Arms and the Cardiff Arms all in the main street. There are two chapels, Penuel Welsh Baptist and Babell Welsh Calvinistic Methodist. It was once a borough, governed by a Portreeve, aldermen and burgesses. It was then the custom that each newly elected burgess prove his fitness for office by draining, in one go, the Corporation horn filled with a pint and a half of strong Welsh ale.

St Llawddog's Church is 19th century with the exception of the 13th century tower. Llawddog lived in the 6th-7th century and is thought to have been the son of Dingad ab Nudd Hael, King of Bryn Buga (Usk). He is associated with Caernarvonshire and Bardsey Island and many miracles were attributed to him. His cult was strong in this area with a well and church at Cenarth and churches at Penboyr and Llanllawddog in Carmarthenshire dedicated to him. In the graveyard is a stone dating from the 6th century with the Ogham inscription 'Trenagusu Maqi Maqitreni', and a Latin inscription, 'Trenegussi Fili Macutreni Hic Iacit'. There is also the grave of and a memorial to Sir William Edward Logan. Logan was born in Montreal in Canada in 1798. Educated at Edinburgh University, in 1831 he became manager of a copper works in Swansea and published a geological map of the South Wales Coalfield. In 1842 he was commissioned to establish the Geological Survey of Canada and remained in charge until 1869. Mount Logan, Canada's highest mountain was named after him, as was the mineral Weloganite and the Geological Association of Canada still awards the Logan Medal. He was a recipient of the French Legion of honour and was knighted in 1856. He retired to Cilgerran in 1869 and died in 1875.

Another resident of Cilgerran was Dr Thomas Phaer, 1510-1560. Born in Norwich, Phaer had studied law at Oxford but it as a doctor of medicine and translator that he is best known. He was perhaps the first paediatrician, identifying various childhood ailments, including 'apostume of the brayne' (meningitis), colic, 'terrible dreames and feare in the slepe' (nightmares) and 'pissing in the bedde' (bedwetting). He is represented in the Coat of Arms of The Royal College of Paediatrics and Child Health. He wrote *The Boke of Children* in 1545, *Natura Brevium* in 1535, and *Newe Boke of Presidentes* in 1543, *The Regiment of Life* in 1544, a translation of a French version of the Latin text *Regimen Sanitatis Salerni.* He complained that doctors described illnesses in Latin to confuse patients. He also translated the first nine books of Virgil's *Aeneid* before his death. He also wrote a biography of Owain Glyndwr, published in the *Mirror for Magistrates* in 1559. He had married Ann, the daughter of Thomas Walter, Alderman of Carmarthen and was Member of Parliament for Carmarthen Boroughs in 1547 and for Cardigan 1555-59. He is buried in the church and his epitaph was written in Latin by Sir Thomas Chaloner.

Cilgerran was on the Whitland to Cardigan Railway, the 'Cardi Bach' and the line ran to the south of the village with Kilgerran Station opposite the Masons Arms. Opened in 1886 it closed in 1962 and the site is now a warehouse. To the north of the village the old track is now used as a footpath as far as the Welsh Wildlife Centre on the Teifi Marshes.

Cilgwyn

Cilgwyn is a small scattered hamlet two miles south-east of Newport. There is a candle maker and a small candle museum.

Situated in a small valley, Mynydd Carningli lies to the west with its cairns, hut circles and Iron Age hill fort.

Formerly a chapelry, the little church of St Mary has undergone a recent renovation and is now a private dwelling.

Cilrhedyn

Part of an old parish, most of which lies in Carmarthenshire, the hamlet of Cilrhedyn lies four miles south of Cenarth on the border with Carmarthenshire. Dominated by a large farm and a plant and machinery company, the countryside is pleasing but there is little of interest. The parish church, which was dedicated to St Teilo, is no longer. It stood adjacent to Tymawr Farm. Still standing is St Teilo's Stone, a four and a half foot tall stone, thought to have been part of a churchyard cross with Ogham inscription, though there is now no trace of that. The parish, which takes in part of Cwm Cych and the valley of the Afon Pedron, was described by Fenton as one of the most pleasing spots in the whole principality.

Clarbeston

Clarbeston is a small agricultural village north-east of Haverfordwest. It is dominated by four large farms with only a few other houses and the parish church of St Martin of Tours. The church was rebuilt in 1841, but little remains of the earlier building.

Clarbeston Road

Clarbeston Road by contrast to Clarbeston is a much larger village, clustered around the railway station on the main Fishguard line. There has been a considerable amount of new housing, though insufficient to maintain the two inns, with the Picton having closed leaving the Cross Inn still open. There are some older cottages in the village but Penuel Methodist Chapel established in 1886 was rebuilt in 1960. There is also Bethany Free Church.

Clarbeston Road is a junction on the railway with one line going to Neyland and the other to Fishguard. Although the intention in the 1840s was for a line to Fishguard, this was dropped in favour of a link to Milford Haven which opened in 1856. The Clarbeston Road to Fishguard line only opened in 1906. It is single track with a passing loop at Letterston. Intermediate stations between Clarbeston Road and Fishguard were closed in 1963.

A little under a mile to the south-east of the village is Lamborough Camp, an Iron Age fortification with a footpath running past.

Clunderwen

Clunderwen is a village, formerly in Carmarthenshire and spelt Clynderwen, on the A478 north of Narberth where the road crosses the rail line to Milford Haven and Fishguard. Originally an agricultural community, it has expanded greatly, with new housing, mainly ribbon development, but with small developments off the main road. It retains its links with agriculture through merchants, but is now a commuting village. It is large enough to sustain a village shop, chemist and hairdresser and the Iron Duke Hotel next to the station.

There is a chapel of ease in the village, built in 1860. It is a small plain building accessed by a lane next to a garage on the A478. Golwg yr Eglwys (Church View) is a small development of bungalows next to the chapel.

There is a camping and caravanning site off Gower Villa Lane.

The Roman road, the Via Julia, ran to the south of the village and is visible as a crop mark at Bryn Hyfryd Farm.

The village was named after Clynderwen Farm, situated to the north-east. Clunderwen means Oak Meadow.

Clydey (Clydau)

The parish of Clydey lies in the north of the county three and a half miles south of Abercych. The village is tiny, with the church in the wooded Cwm Cneifa, dedicated to St Clydai, a saint thought to be one of the many sainted children of Brychan, the king of what is now Breconshire. The church is built in a traditional Welsh *llan* or circular church ground and is 13th-14th century with a battlemented tower. There are three stones now kept inside the church with inscriptions dating from the 5th century. All three have Latin texts while two also have Ogham script.

Coedcanlas

Coedcanlas was a parish and hamlet on the eastern shore of Beggars Reach on the Daucleddau. Coedcanlas Farm was the birthplace of jockey and author Dick Francis. Lewis in 1833 noted that the church was a small picturesque building of great antiquity, recently repaired at the expense of Sir John Owen. Even in 1833, St Mary's was rarely used for divine service and is now a roofless ruin near Chapel Cottages.

Cold Blow

Cold Blow was the site of a cross roads and a gate on the turnpike road from Narberth, two miles to the north-west, and Tenby to Tavernspite and Carmarthen. The listing in *Leigh's New Pocket Road-Book of England and Wales* of 1833 as being 236½ miles from the Tyburn Turnpike, gives some idea of the importance of this junction in the early 19th century. A stagecoach ran three times a week to Tenby during the summer season, connecting with the mail coach. There were just a few houses around the cross roads before late 20th century developments and the establishment of a camping and caravanning site. According to Charles Henry Hartsholme, writing in 1841, the prefix 'cold' appears to predominate near Roman settlements and he states that there are three places known as Cold Blow in Pembrokeshire, though he makes no mention of Cold Inn.

Cold Inn

A hamlet two miles west of Saundersfoot, which despite the name has no inn. Cold Inn is still small despite new housing outnumbering the few older cottages. The road through the village would have been the old stage route before 1839 when the turnpike road was built; it is likely that there was an inn and in 1755 it was known as New Inn.

Cold Inn was once the centre of small scale anthracite mining, but all trace of this industry has disappeared.

Cosheston

Cosheston is an attractive village, two miles east of Pembroke Dock. There are some 18th century houses in the centre of the village which has expanded greatly in recent years with individual developments. The Brewery Inn and Restaurant has attractive Victorian arched windows, though the building is much older.

The church of St Michael and All Angels, is on an elevated site on Point Lane. It is medieval in origin and has been extended and largely rebuilt over the years with a slim, battlemented bell tower and double aisle.

To the south of the village the medieval strip field system is still in use.

Cosheston Hall, to the north of the village dates back to before 1556 when it was sold to the Rossant family. The present building is 19th century. Paskeston Hall, to the east of the village was owned by the Roche family and is now open for Victorian Country House teas. Bangeston Hall is to the west of Cosheston and is now a care home specializing in autism. It is a 19th century house, not to be confused with Bangeston, near Angle which was derelict in Fenton's time. Named after the Norman Beneger family, Ralph Beneger rebuilt Pwllcrochan Church in 1342. The connection of the Beneger family with Bangeston Hall is unclear.

Cresswell Quay

Cresswell Quay was used for shipping coal in the 18th and early 19th centuries. Situated on the Cresswell River, it is today a quiet hamlet with its main attraction the Cresselly Arms. The village was originally called Christ's Well Chapel, no doubt referring to the ruined Cresswell Castle on the opposite bank of the Cresswell, which was a 13th century defensive building occupied by the Augustinian Priory at Haverfordwest. The Georgian Cresswell House overlooking the river is now a bed and breakfast establishment.

To the north is Cresswell Corn Mill, now converted into accommodation, but, according to Coflein, with the machinery and water wheel intact.

Cresselly

Cresselly is dominated by Cresselly House, the home of the Allen family since 1728 when John Allen married Joan Bartlet. It was previously in the hands of the Bartlet family from 1564. Fenton stayed there in 1809 when he described it as "an elegant seat standing on a very elevated spot, and though in the midst of a colliery, yet is so judiciously screened by plantations from the sight of those dingy volcanoes so often thrown up, that the front, in which are the principal sitting rooms, takes in nothing that can remind you of them; but looks down Cresswell River to that most beautifully object Lawrenny, and its woods terminating the vista; a prospect even when the tide is out, not disagreeable, being at a competent distance, but when full in, exhibiting a scene remarkably pleasing and lively from the small craft perpetually on the wing, either coming up or going down to and from Cresswell."

Today Georgian Cresswell House is owned by Hugh Harrison-Allen and is open for bed and breakfast and if pre-booked, dinner. The house was built in 1770 with additional wings added in the 1860s. The gardens are 19th century with a walled kitchen garden.

Just over 600 yards to the east of Cresselly House is the Primitive Methodist Chapel, established in 1837 and rebuilt in Gothic style in 1893. Mounds in the fields locally are remnants of the coal industry.

The name Cresselly is believed to have been derived from *cres* and *gelli*, meaning a parched grove, possibly because of the coal in the area.

Crinow

Crinow is a small village near Narberth. In Welsh 'Crynwedd' the derivation of the name is not clear. It consists of a single lane which is a no through road with the redundant little parish church towards the end of the lane. According to Owen the church was formerly called Llandeilo Velfrey. Lewis in 1849 reported: "The church is a very small edifice, without tower or spire; but of late years it has been repaired and beautified, and rendered one of the neatest churches in the county. A Sunday school is supported by Miss Eaton".

The churchyard is now a 'living churchyard', with hedgehogs, bats, frogs and insects being encouraged. The church is small with nave chancel, western bellcote and southern porch. Plans from 1840 show that there was a raised gallery at the western end of the nave but this disappeared in a later restoration. There are a number of attractive older houses and the Georgian country house of Parc Glas, formerly the home of Roger Eaton.

Croes-goch

On the A4791 St David's to Fishguard road Croes-Goch (Red Cross) is on a cross roads. There is a mix of old and new buildings. The Artramont Arms is on the crossroads and takes its name from the Artramont estate in County Wexford in Ireland. Artramont was established by the De la Rupes of Roche Castle in the 12th century but was granted to the Le Hunte family by Cromwell. Following troubles in Ireland, the family moved to Pembrokeshire where they had substantial estates and were connected through marriage with the prominent families of the county. Opposite the inn is the gallery and studio of John Knapp Fisher, a well known Pembrokeshire artist, housed in a single storey cottage.

To the west of the village on Felinwent Farm is Parc y Battles, believed to be the site of a battle, the blood from which gave the village its name. When building the houses in Mor Awel, an early cemetery was discovered with cist burials. Carbon dating has attributed the burials to AD 600 or earlier.

Croes Goch is on elevated ground with the sea in the distance. There are the sites of two windmills, one either side of the road to St David's. The Welsh Baptist Chapel was established in 1816.

The village has a modern bi-lingual junior school.

Crosswell

Crosswell is a small hamlet on crossroads one and a half miles south-west of Eglwyswrw. The name suggests the existence of a well, and there is the village pump right on the cross. There are four modern bungalows and some attractive older houses and cottages.

Crunwere

Crunwere is an ancient parish in the south-east corner of Pembrokeshire. The Welsh name of Cronwern means 'Circular Alder Grove'. There is no village, but the now redundant parish church, dedicated to St Elidyr, lies to the north of the A477, signposted near the village of Llanteg. The nave and chancel date from the 13th century with the 16th century tower. Further building took place in the mid 19th century when the church was renovated. There are some good stained glass windows dating from 1878 with further additions in the 1950s.

Crymych

Crymych, a large village on the A478, owes its existence to the coming of the railway. In 1880, the Whitland to Cardigan line, known as the Cardi Bach, opened with a station at Crymych. The village developed as a commercial centre for the agricultural community in the area, a role which continues long after the closure of the railway.

The Welsh language comprehensive school for the area now dominates the village which has a range of shops and agricultural merchants as well as two chapels and the Crymych Arms Hotel. There is continued housing development on the outskirts of the village, while the old railway station yard is now a small industrial area.

Crymych is a centre for touring the Preseli Hills and the sources of the Afon Taf and Afon Gafel both lie within the village. The Cardi Bach followed the Taf as far as Crymych and then cut through to the southern slopes of the Teifi valley.

At the end of Llain Drigarn (Three Cairns Space) is an undisturbed barrow, shown as a tumulus on the Ordnance Survey map.

One and a half miles west of the village is Foel Trigarn, an Iron Age hill fort named after the three cairns at the summit. Situated on the eastern ridge of Mynydd Preseli it occupies one of the most spectacular sites of all the Iron Age forts in Wales. There is evidence that no less than 227 houses were built within the walls, forming in effect a local tribal centre. The cairns pre-date the fort, being Bronze Age. South-west along on the ridge is another cairn some 50 feet across.

A little under a mile and a half north-east of Crymych is the mountain of Frenni Fawr. Wirt Sikes in his 1880 book *British Goblins* relates the legend of the Fairies of Frenni Fawr. (*Tylwyth Teg* is Welsh for Fair Folk or fairies) "About ten miles south of Cardigan is the Pembrokeshire mountain called Frennifawr, which is the scene of this tale: A shepherd's lad was tending his sheep on the small mountains called Frennifach one fine morning in June. Looking to the top of Frennifawr to note what way the fog hung – for if the fog on that mountain hangs on the Pembrokeshire side, there will be fair weather, if on the Cardigan side, storm – he saw the *Tylwyth Teg*, in appearance like tiny soldiers, dancing in a ring. He set out for the scene of revelry, and soon drew near the ring where, in a gay company of males and females, they were footing it to the music of the harp. Never had he seen such handsome people, nor any so enchantingly cheerful. They beckoned him with laughing faces to join them as they leaned backward almost falling, whirling round and round with joined hands. Those who were dancing never swerved from the perfect circle; but some were clambering over the old cromlech, and others chasing each other with surprising swiftness and the greatest glee. Still others rode about on small white horses of the most beautiful form; these riders were little ladies, and their dresses were indescribably elegant, surpassing the sun in radiance, and varied in colour, some being of bright whiteness, others the most vivid scarlet. The males wore red tripled caps, and the ladies a light fantastic headdress which waved in the wind. All this was in silence, for the shepherd could not hear the harps, though he saw them. But now he drew nearer to the circle, and finally ventured to put his foot in the magic ring. The instant he did this, his ears were charmed with strains of the most melodious music he had ever heard. Moved with the transports this seductive harmony produced in him, he stepped fully into the ring. He was no sooner in than he found himself in a palace glittering with gold and pearls. Every form of beauty surrounded him, and every variety of pleasure was offered him. He was made free to range whither he would, and his every movement was waited on by young women of the most matchless loveliness. And no tongue can tell the joys of feasting that were his! Instead of the *tatws-a-llaeth* (potatoes and buttermilk) to which he had hitherto been accustomed, here were birds and meats of every choice description, served on plates of silver. Instead of home-brewed *cwrw* (beer), the only bacchic beverage he had ever tasted in real life, here were red and yellow wines of wondrous enjoyableness, brought in golden goblets richly inlaid with gems. The waiters were the most beautiful virgins, and everything was in abundance. There was but one restriction on his freedom: he must not drink, on any consideration, from a certain well in the garden, in which swam fishes of every colour, including the colour of gold. Each day new joys were provided for his amusement, new scenes of beauty were unfolded to him, new faces presented themselves, more lovely if possible than those he had before encountered. Everything was done to charm him; but one day all his happiness fled in an instant. Possessing every joy that mortal could desire, he wanted the one thing forbidden – like Eve in the garden, like Fatima in the castle; curiosity undid him. He plunged his hand into the well: the fishes all disappeared instantly. He put the water to his mouth: a confused shriek ran through the garden. He drank: the palace and all vanished from his sight, and he stood shivering in the night air, alone on the mountain, in the very place where he had first entered the ring."

Another legend of Frenni Fawr tells of a hidden leaden casket full with 'untold gold', guarded by a spirit hat takes the form of "a violent tempest, which bursts, in thunder and lightning, around the head of the man who is foolhardy enough to seek to possess himself of the forbidden prize."

Cuffern

Described by Fenton as a "handsome modern mansion", Cuffern Manor Country House today is a guest house set in three and a half acres of grounds, one and a quarter miles east of Roch. Woodlands is a chalet park and East Moor Park is a somewhat incongruous development deep in the heart of rural Pembrokeshire, consisting of 65 two- and three-bedroom retirement homes with leisure facilities and a resident warden.

Cwm-yr-Eglwys (Church Valley)

Cwm yr Eglwys is a pretty village south-east of Dinas Head in north Pembrokeshire. The village is approached by a narrow road with steep hedges and is a favourite with boat owners and holidaymakers with a safe sandy beach and slipway protected by Dinas Island from the prevailing south-westerly winds. Dinas is not an island, but the valley between Cwm yr Eglwys and Pwllgwaelod effectively cuts off the 'island', the only buildings on which are at Island Farm.

There is limited parking and boat storage in the village together with a small caravan park.

At the beach is the graveyard and ruined church of St Brynach, a 12th century church destroyed by the Royal Charter Storm of 1859 and further damaged in 1979. Only the west wall and belfry remain. The 12th century church replaced an earlier, probably wooden church destroyed by Viking raiders. The 1859 storm was named after the *Royal Charter* which sank off the coast of Anglesey with the loss of 450 lives. She was one of 133 ships which sank during the storm which raged over several days travelling up the west coast from Cornwall to Scotland. 100 mile an hour winds were measured, causing widespread damage.

The first two weeks of August see a regatta organized by the local boat club.

Dale

Dale is situated on the eastern coast of the peninsular to the north of the entrance to Milford Haven. As such it enjoys protection from the south-westerly gales. Dale was once a borough, probably known as Vale after the knight Sir Robert De Vale who was granted a weekly market and annual fair at his manor. In the 18th century there were no less than 18 inns, but Dale's remoteness led to its decline and today it is an attractive village with narrow streets and a good selection of old buildings at its heart. 1950s and 60s housing on Blue Anchor Way failed to anticipate the general increase in car ownership with the resulting lack of garages and parking spaces.

The heart of the village has good car parks and facilities for boat owners, with a slipway and jetty opposite the Boathouse. The beach is a Blue Flag beach, though not the best in Pembrokeshire in terms of its sands. The main attraction is for yachting, boating and windsurfing, while there is a dive boat and other boats offering sea fishing and sightseeing trips. Westdale Bay across the peninsular offers better sands but is less accessible.

The Griffin Inn is on the sea front as is the Moorings restaurant and the Boathouse café. The last house to the south of the seafront is the former Brig Inn, which Timmins says "bears evident traces of its smuggler patrons, being literally honeycombed with cellars and secret cupboards for the storage of their booty. Even now the walls still reek with moisture, from the salt stored away in inaccessible corners during those piping times when that commodity was worth a couple of guineas the hundredweight."

The present Dale Castle was built as a private house in 1910 but incorporates some of the original Norman castle. The De Vales were succeeded as owners by the Walters of Roch, and a portrait of Lucy Walters, a lover of Charles II and mother of the Duke of Monmouth was known to hang in the castle. In the early 19th century it was the home of the Lloyd family of Cardiganshire and then through marriage to the Philipps family. In the grounds is the four foot high Martyr's Stone, said to have been moved here from Haverfordwest where it marked the site of the burning at the stake of William Nichol in 1558 in the reign of Mary Tudor.

Dale church, dedicated to St James, stands near the Castle and is medieval in origin with a 15th century tower and considerable Victorian restoration, leaving only the east and north walls from the original building.

At Dale Point, south of the bay, is Dale Fort. First established in Elizabethan times, it was used as a defensive position and Royal Observer Corps site until 1946 and has a number of gun emplacements. It is now used as a field study centre run by the Field Studies Council with students and other researchers studying the shore and marine environment. It has its own small slipway.

At the southern end of Dale Peninsular is St Anne's Head and just to the east Mill Bay. It was here on 7th August, 1485 that Henry Tudor, Earl of Richmond, landed before marching to the Battle of Bosworth on 22nd August where he defeated Richard III and took the crown as Henry VII. While Henry landed at Mill Bay, his 55 ships and 4000 men sailed round to Dale and disembarked there. The event is commemorated annually in Dale.

At St Anne's Head there is the old lighthouse dating from 1800, itself replacing an earlier coal fired light, known as the high light, which was in use until 1910 and now has an observation platform. The other lighthouse, known as the low light, is still operational. It was built in 1841, replacing a building of 1800. There are a number of coastguard cottages as well as a helipad and the Trinity House building. It is thought that the lighthouse was built on the site of St Anne's Chapel. Already a ruin in the reign of Elizabeth I, the chapel was, according to Owen, an important landmark for shipping entering the Haven.

To the north-west of Dale is the wartime Dale airbase. At first used for bombers by the RAF, it was taken over by the Fleet Air Arm. All around the coast are relics of former defensive buildings and gun emplacements, signifying the strategic importance of the entrance to the Haven.

Dinas Cross – City Cross

Dinas Cross is a village on the A487 Fishguard to Newport road. A ribbon development stretching along the main road with roads running off to Bryn Henllan, Cwm yr Eglwys and the beaches of the north Pembrokeshire coast. It is in effect a number of hamlets. There is a good mix of old cottages and houses as well as modern building. Part has a village green while around the turning to Bryn yr Eglwys there are two pubs and a number of shops. The village also has its own blacksmith.

There are two standing stones. The Lady Stone is adjacent to the main road immediately after the 40 mile an hour sign coming from Fishguard. Standing a little over eight foot, this pointed stone was so named because it resembled a veiled woman. Parc Cerrig Hirion stone stands just under seven foot high and is in a field behind the Mercury Garage. There is also a defensive enclosure and a walled water pump.

Above the village is Bwlch Mawr, a high point with a car park offering superb views across Dinas Island.

In the corner of a field to the north of the road a mile and a half towards Newport is Cerri y Gof, a Neolithic burial chamber of a design unseen elsewhere. A set of five chambers are set in the outer edge of a 35 foot diameter mound and face outwards. Pottery, bones, charcoal and pebbles were found in 19th century excavations.

Dreenhill

A hamlet a little over a mile south-west of the outskirts of Haverfordwest, Dreenhill has a garage and inn, the Masons Arms, on the main road. To the south, next to Croft Farm is the pretty little Methodist Chapel, now converted to a private dwelling.

There are the remains of a fort in Denant Woods to the east of Denant Farm, while further south, half a mile from the village, is Denant Mill, now a private residence, it was built in 1592 and operated until the 1950s.

Druidston

Fenton gives the name as Drewson, being a corruption of Druidstown. The earliest reference is Drewyston meaning Drew's Farm in 1393, but the 19th century antiquaries insisted on a druidical link and today the Druidston name is used. The most likely derivation is from the knight Alfred Drue who is known to have signed several grants to religious houses in the reign of Henry I. The hamlet is inland from St Bride's Bay and consists of farms. The interesting features are on the coast road from Nolton to Broad Haven. Druidston Haven has a superb beach with the small Druidstone Hotel on the cliffs to the south. Above the beach is Malador, an earth house built into the landscape by Future Systems in 1994. Known locally as the 'Teletubbies House'.

In the field east of the hotel are two monoliths. Fenton in 1810 reported that there was "a remarkable inclosure, occupying near an acre of ground, called Drewson Chapel. The stones that composed the druidical circle were removed in 1740 to build with, so there is scarce anything left to mark the situation of this spacious Gorsedd."

Mary Morgan relates the story of an American ship that was wrecked here. Amongst its cargo was gunpowder and one man was so annoyed with the eagerness of the locals to pillage, he smashed a musket against a rock and the resulting spark caused an explosion that killed and maimed a large number of the wreckers.

East Williamston

East Williamston is a pleasant village which has seen rapid expansion in recent years, with mainly individual new houses. Situated just four miles north-west of Tenby it was a chapelry of Begelly, with the chapel described as in a sorry state in the 1840s. The parish church of St Elidyr now sits down a lane near Church Farm. The church was built in 1880 on the foundations of the old chapel and the tower was added. The bowl of the font is Norman. An additional burial ground was purchased in 1898 from the Philipps family.

Until 1839, the village was on the route of the Royal Mail Coach from Carmarthen to Pembroke, but in that year the turnpike road that is now the A477 opened, bypassing East Williamston.

From the 17th century coal has been mined here, though deeper mining techniques saw the collieries move to the Broadmoor area and the last pit in the village closed early in the 19th century.

There is a small village green with a modern community hall.

There is still evidence of the Norman strip field system around East Williamston, though many fields have been amalgamated.

Eglwyswen – Whitechurch

Eglwyswen is a former parish in north Pembrokeshire, two and a half miles north-west of Crymych. The church of St Michael stands on its own, hidden from the road by trees. Of medieval origin, it was dedicated to St Meugen until 1786. Originally white, it was rebuilt in the 19th century but has been deconsecrated and is now a private dwelling. The churchyard however is still owned by the Church in Wales.

George Owen remarked that in Tudor times the locals were particularly good at chess!

Nearby is Plas Whitechurch, a substantial farm house that was formerly a mid 18th century gentleman's residence.

Eglwyswrw

Eglwyswrw is a village on the A487 Fishguard to Cardigan road. The name denotes the church of St Wrw, or Eirw or Gwrw, whose body was said to have been interred in a chantry chapel in the church. Sabine-Gould found no information on this saint, not even the gender. It is an old village with some modern development. The church of St Christiolus is medieval in origin with substantial 19th century renovation, set in a Celtic *llan*. A chapel and holy well were apparently destroyed in the reign of Elizabeth I on the orders of the Privy Council as it was frequented by Catholics.

The village has a shop and the Butcher's Arms, but the Sergeant's Arms Inn opposite the church is now a private house. The inn was so-named because the court officers gathered there when the court was in session in the old courthouse next door. At the rear of the Sergeant's Arms is an early 19th century meeting house, later used as a school, chapel and church hall and now sandwiched between two modern houses.

Malkin describes that a shopkeeper in Eglwyswrw by the name of Evans had, by 1803, made a fortune by honest industry. He was doing business in banking of £20,000 a year and procuring books and any specified articles from London for the local residents.

There are the remnants of a motte and bailey castle to the north of the main road, at the 30 mph sign entering from the west. There is also a holy spring dedicated to St Mary which has been modernised.

Two thirds of a mile north-west of the village was Court, a moated house, one of the residences of David Martin, the bishop of St David's, at the beginning of the 14th century. Three sides of the rock cut moat remain.

To the west of Eglwyswrw are three Iron Age hill forts, at Castell Llwyd, Castell Mawr and south of Castell Mawr on the banks of the Afon Nyfer. Castell Mawr, which is the most easily identifiable, was considered by some to have been an earlier ritual henge, taken over as a fort in the Iron Age. It is one and a half miles from Eglwyswrw.

Just over half a mile west of the village is the Dyfed Shire Horse Farm Park which has a range of animals, play areas and a café.

One and a half miles west of Eglwyswrw, to the north of the main road, is Castell Henllys, a reconstructed Iron Age settlement within an Iron Age fort. Using materials available at the time, four round houses have been built on their original foundations enabling visitors to experience life in Britain as it was 2500 years ago.

Eglwyswrw was combined with the parish of Meline and the church of St Dogmael, Meline is situated just 330 yards south of Castell Henllys. The church was rebuilt in the 1860s and has a possibly unique window in the form of a Star of David. It was a gift from a Jewish family who were allowed to worship in the church on a Saturday. The chancel is unusual for this area in that the east wall is in the form of an apse with three windows, two plain while the third has a single light stained glass image of the crucifixion with the Virgin Mary and St John and the inscription 'By thy cross and passion good Lord deliver us'. There is a small bellcote with weathervane above.

To the south-east of the village is Castell Llainfawr, a set of earthworks thought to have been a medieval castle.

Felindre Farchog /Velindre

Felindre Farchog, The Place of the Knight's Mill, is a pretty hamlet on the A471 Fishguard to Cardigan road. The Salutation Inn is now a large establishment with a separate restaurant and a beer garden alongside the Afon Nyfer.

The grey stone building at the north-eastern end of the village is Llys Dy, from the 1860s to 1976, the courthouse of the Lord of Cenmaes.

Pentre Ifan

Dating from 1626, the building had its Gothic conversion in 1852 when it was converted for use as a college by George Owen, but he died before completing the alterations. It became a private dwelling and was modernised in 2000. Across the Moylgrove road from Llys Dy is a circular enclosure, used for stray animals.

The Cana Independent Chapel was built in 1857, replacing Yr Hen Capel of 1810. The latter is now Cana Vestry, 50 yards away on the opposite side of the road from the chapel.

A quarter of a mile out of the village the Cardigan road crosses the Nant Duad. The early bridge was known as Pont Baldwin, after Archbishop Baldwin who toured Wales in 1188 to recruit for the Third Crusade preached there. It was widened in 1910.

A mile and a quarter south of Felindre Farchog is Pentre Ifan, described as the finest Neolithic Tomb in Wales. The uprights are up to eight foot high and support a capstone of 16 tons. Significantly the stones which formed the forecourt of the now disappeared mound which covered the tomb remain in place. Built 6000 years ago this wild and remote site is well worth a visit.

Folly

Folly is a small hamlet north of Camrose. Five roads meet at Folly Cross and there is Folly Farm, but no apparent reason for the name. The Folly Farm here has nothing to do with the Folly Farm Theme Park near Begelly.

Freshwater East

Freshwater East is a village built above the bay on the south Pembrokeshire coast. Almost exclusively a 20th century development, it has the Freshwater Inn on Jason Road with a large garden overlooking the sea. North of the village, off Chapel Lane, are the remains of the 15th century St Mary's Chapel. To the south of Jason Road are the earthworks of an Iron Age defensive enclosure.

The beach is good and sandy, backed by dunes and cliffs. There is a Caravan Club site and the Freshwater Holiday Village, offering self-catering accommodation.

It is a popular surfing beach with large challenging Winter breakers.

Portclew House north of the village is a three storey Georgian Country House set in gardens. It is now a guest house also offering self-catering accommodation in the various converted out-buildings.

Freystrop

Freystrop is an ancient parish some two miles south of Haverfordwest, with St Justinian's church at Little Milford. The name has connotations of Norse mythology, where Freya was the goddess of love and fertility. Originally the bulk of the population lived at Lower Freystrop, but modern development has seen the growth of Freystrop Cross where there was just one cottage in 1733. In the 18th century there was small scale coal mining in the area which expanded in the 19th century, changing the nature of the settlement. All evidence of mining has disappeared, though the quay at nearby Hook would have been used for shipping coal.

Peregrine Phillips was vicar of Freystrop during the time of Cromwell. A celebrated puritan, he was riding home after dark when his horse fell into a coal pit and became stuck. Phillips'cries for assistance were heard by the son of a local deaf woman and he was rescued by the mine owner. After the restoration of the Monarchy, Phillips refused to accept the *Book of Common Prayer* and was ejected from the parish though he was given accommodation at nearby Dredgman Hill Farm, the property of Sir Herbert Perrot, which he used as an Independent House Church. Phillips is buried near the pulpit of Haroldstone church.

In 1847 inspectors reported on the local school which was funded by local gentry and farmers, so that rent of £3 and a salary of £12 was paid annually. Education was free save for the cost of coal in winter. The school teacher was an elderly Mr Thomas Henry Davies who it was reported could not speak English correctly. Arithmetic was not taught.

Bethel Congregational Church is at Middle Hill, between Lower Freystrop and Freystrop Cross. It was built in 1819, with rebuilds in 1840 and 1884.

South of Freystrop Cross is Clareston Mansion, originally home to the Powel family but passing through marriage to the Roch family who modernized the house at the start of the 19th century. It is now a farm.

Near the entrance to Clareston is the Puddleduck Bridge and Puddleduck Trout Fishery. The old bridge has now been bypassed, but the old road can be accessed just south of Clayston Grove.

Gethsemane (See Nevern)

Glanrhyd

A small hamlet on the B4582 north-east of Nevern, the settlement is dominated by the Calvinistic Methodist Chapel built in 1807 and rebuilt in 1870. The chapel was built at the side of a ford, crossing a tributary of Nant Ceibwr. The former primary school serving Llantood is now the home and workshop of Jonathan Guest, furniture designer and maker.

Glogue

Glogue is a hamlet in rural north Pembrokeshire two and a quarter miles south-east of Crymych. There is a terrace of houses which would until 1962 have looked out over the Whitland to Cardigan Railway line. The houses were almost certainly built to accommodate workers at the nearby slate quarry. The line follows the Afon Taf and to the north-west of the Terrace stood Glogue Station. Station House and the crossing gate are the only remnants of the station, but the track is now a footpath, leading south to Llanfyrnach and north-west to Crymych. The line opened in 1875 and there was a siding to Glogue slate quarry, once one of the largest in the county. The quarry closed in 1926.

The hamlet takes its name from Glogue Farm, Glogue being an Anglicized form of *Y Glog*, meaning a rock or precipice.

Granston

Granston is a tiny village north of the St David's to Fishguard road. The church of St Catherine is largely 19th century though on a much older site. The church has a simple nave and chancel with a north transept and porch and a west bellcote. Built on a hill it is now part of a pilgrimage route.

Half a mile west of the church is Tregwynt Mansion, once the home of the Harries family, it was the site of a hoard of coins from the English Civil War discovered in 1996. The hoard is now in the British Museum. It consisted of 33 gold and 467 silver coins and a gold posie ring. The Mansion was the scene of a ball in 1797 when news of the French invasion came through. Today Tregwynt is a music and exhibition venue.

Gumfreston

A tiny hamlet two and a half miles from Tenby on the B4318, Gumfreston has a little gem of a 12th century church. Dedicated to St Lawrence, there are three holy wells in the churchyard, two are chalybeate, containing iron, and naturally sparkling. All have stonework and are thought to have been the site of a pre-Christian well cult. Gumfreston itself was a minor place of pilgrimage and at one time the building of a pump room was contemplated. Timmins in 1895 noted the remains of a cock fighting pit near the wells.

Apparently Easter Monday was the day for such activities. The church tower was originally separate from the church but is now an integral part. The medieval altar stone is now part of the flooring but its inscribed crosses are still visible. On the north wall are the remains of an early painting of Christ, with craft tools used locally, thought to symbolise the evil of working on a Sunday.

The name Gumfreston derives from a Norse settler named Gomfre or Gumfrid.

Gumfreston was once a much larger village, with the now dry estuary of the Ritec, to the west, suitable for shipping. It was a crossing point for travellers to Ireland and for pilgrims to St David's. The estuary was drained when the Penally embankment was built between Tenby and Penally, in 1811, by John Owen (knighted in 1813) of Orielton to provide more farmland. The embankment later carried the railway line from Tenby to Pembroke.

Today most of the small hamlet lies to the north of the main road, but consists of less than a dozen houses. To the south of the main road is St Lawrence Country Guest House, the former Old Rectory, overlooking the Ritec Valley with St Lawrence Church in its grounds.

On the opposite side of the main road to the church is a farmhouse that Timmins reports to being one of the oldest buildings in the county. "Out from the main structure projects a mighty porch, running up the full height of the house, and pierced with round holes by way of windows above the main doorway. The place is built as though intended to last for all time, and is enveloped in the customary coating of weather-stained whitewash." During my visit, there were signs of renovation, but the round windows were still there and the porch had a pink wash. The gable end of the little building next door is pierced with pigeon holes.

Haroldston West

Haroldston West is situated north of Broad Haven. A small community, there is evidence of an earlier, larger settlement. There is now a holiday village consisting of timber chalets, known as Timber Hill, in the valley leading down from Haroldston Farm.

St Madoc's church, a small church with belfry set in a hollow, has recently been renovated. It is thought that there has been a church here since the 6th century.

Harold Stone which gives the settlement its name is a Bronze Age stone some six foot high, standing behind St Catherine's bungalow, but visible from the Coastal Path. According to Giraldus Cambrensis this was one of the stones erected by Harold around the western coastline of Wales after he had ravaged it, but more recent research attributes it to an earlier period. Some believe that it may have formed part of a stone circle, but there are the remains of a stone circle at Upper Lodge nearer to Broad Haven and it is unlikely that this stone was part of a circle.

Lower Haroldston or East Haroldston

Lower Haroldston is an old parish on the banks of the Cleddau south of Haverfordwest, believed to have been named after the Harold family who owned Haroldston as early as 1307. The family was believed to be of Norse descent arriving in the area prior to the Norman Conquest. In 1301 Sir William Harold was appointed Constable of Haverfordwest Castle and his grandson was Sir Richard Harold. Haroldston house passed to the Perrot family after the marriage of Alice, daughter of Sir Richard Harold to Peter Perrot, her father's squire. Its most famous owner was Sir John Perrot, believed by some to be the illegitimate son of Henry VIII and Mary Berkeley, who was married to Sir Thomas Perrot. It is said the Sir John bore a remarkable resemblance in appearance, voice and temperament to Henry. Sir John was a favourite of Edward VI but fell out of favour with Mary who accused him of harbouring protestant heretics at Haroldston. He was one of the four canopy bearers at the coronation of Queen Elizabeth I who appointed him Lord Deputy of Ireland. He was gifted Carew and Laugharne Castles and further enlarged the estate by acquiring the lands of the dissolved monastery of Haverfordwest. He eventually fell out of favour and was convicted of treason. The queen however refused to sign his death warrant and he died in the Tower. Elizabeth I restored the bulk of his estates to his son. The Perrot family remained at Haroldston which became the social hub of the county. Joseph Addison, the founder with Richard Steele of the *Spectator*, was a frequent visitor and it is said that he got the idea for his character Sir Roger de Coverley from Sir Herbert Perrot. Addison met his wife, the Dowager Duchess of Warwick at Haroldston. Sir Herbert's daughter, Hester, inherited the estate and married Sir John Pakington. They left Haroldston which fell into decay. By 1810, when Fenton visited, it was already in ruins.

The little church of St Ishmael is next to Lower Haroldston Farm. The nave with its bellcote dates from the 13th century, as does the font. The porch and chancel are later. Near the pulpit is the tomb of Peregrine Phillips, the celebrated puritan preacher of Pembrokeshire and former vicar of Freystrop. The church was associated with St Caradoc the hermit who had a cell close by and who is commemorated by St Caradoc's Well which is to be found on the common where Haverfordwest Races were held.

South-west of the church is Fern Hill, the former home of Sir Henry Matthias, Prothonotary of the Carmarthen circuit from 1783 until the Court of Great Sessions was abolished in 1830.

Hasguard

Hasguard today is a farming community centred on Hasguard Cross on the B4327 Haverfordwest to Dale road with its caravan park. The old parish church of St Peter's Hasguard is situated to the south of the crossroads next to Hasguard Farm. Now in ruins, with just the walls and belfry, it stands roofless within the graveyard. It is medieval in origin but was rebuilt in the 19th century. Within is the tomb of Katherine Meyrick, wife of the Bishop of Bangor and mother of Sir Gilly Meyrick who was executed, alongside his lifelong friend the Earl of Essex, at Tower Hill in 1601.

The name Hasguard has a number of explanations, including an enclosure, and 'house cleft' shown as *Huis Skarth* from Scandinavian, referring to the small valley here, though some have attributed it to Asguard, the 'place of bliss' in Norse mythology.

Hayscastle and Hayscastle Cross

Hays Castle was an early Norman motte and bailey castle and the motte remains near the little parish church. It stands at the head of a small valley that runs down to Newgale some three and a half miles to the south-west. The little church of St Mary is 12th century in origin, refurbished in 1927. Hayscastle itself is very small and the main population is to be found at Hayscastle Cross on the B4330. There is the Cross Inn and a few older cottages on the main road with more modern development on the side roads.

Just beyond the Cross on the Letterston road is a disused army camp, to the south of which is a round barrow, now just five feet high.

At Crossways, three quarters of a mile south-west of the Cross, is Hayscastle Tump, the remains of a much excavated and damaged Bronze Age round barrow. A little further west there are further barrows and a standing stone.

Within the parish is Ford, which once had a chapel of ease. Set in a wooded valley just under a mile and a half south-west of Hayscastle, there is now a caravan and camping site where once stood Stoopers Mill and, further down Brandy Brook, a further two mills. Above the valley there are the remains of an Iron Age settlement.

Henry's Moat

Henry's Moat is a small village a quarter of a mile south of Tufton which lies on the B4329 which runs north-east from Haverfordwest. The name is derived from Castell Hen-dref or Old Town Castle. As in New Moat, the terms moat and castle appear to have been interchangeable in Pembrokeshire.

St Brynach's Church is small with 13th-14th century nave and chancel and a simple bellcote. It was refurbished in 1884. The church was in the patronage of the Scourfield family of New Moat.

To the east of the church is the ten foot high motte of the castle which gives the village its name. It is believed to have been a Norman timber motte and bailey castle of the 12th century. Just under 1100 yards to the north-east of the church is St Brynach's Well, a holy well with traces of a medieval chapel. (For details of St Brynach see Llanfyrnach).

Herbrandston

Herbrandston on the north shore of Milford Haven is a village founded by a Fleming named Herbrandt, in the early years of the Norman Conquest. The ancient village with its little church has expanded in recent years from a population of 200 in 1960 to over 1500. It is close to the South Hook LNG (Liquidized Natural Gas) Terminal and the giant Milford Haven Oil Refinery.

Three miles from Milford Haven, Herbrandston has an inn, the Taberna while the church of St Mary is Norman in origin with a squat tower which was lowered in the 18th century. There is the badly worn figure of a knight in the church, while outside is the grave of the only soldier from the village to have died in either world war. He was stabbed to death by a fellow soldier who was acquitted of murder, but it is said that the apparition of a hand holding a dagger is seen on the tomb.

South of the village, now surrounded by the LNG plant, is the South Hook Fort artillery complex, built in the 1860s but abandoned in 1930. A further fort was built on Stack Rock, an island in the Haven which had, in the 1870s, 16 18-ton Rifled Muzzle Loading (RML) guns which were manned by 150 soldiers.

Hill Mountain

Hill Mountain is a village two miles south-east of Freystrop. It is a modern village with mainly new housing built along two roads with two small estates of detached houses between them.

Hodgeston

Hodgeston is an attractive small village a little over a mile south-east of Lamphey. The name is derived from someone called Hogg or Hodge. The church with its slender tower and 14th century chancel built under Bishop de Gower is now owned by the Friends of Friendless Churches. The nave is plain, but the chancel has a richly decorated triple sedilia, piscina and fine traceried windows

North of the church at the junction with the Lamphey road are the remains of a moated platform on which a building stood until 1870.

Thomas Young of Hodgeston was a student and later Principal of Broadgates Hall Oxford before becoming precentor at St David's Cathedral. A Protestant, he went into exile during the reign of Mary Tudor, returning to become Bishop of St David's and in 1561, Archbishop of York. He died in 1568 at the age of 61.

Hook

Hook is a medium sized village on the banks of the Western Cleddau south of Haverfordwest. There has been significant modern development but there are a number of attractive older cottages.

Hook Quay was built, in 1791, by a local man, Caesar Matthias Junior, to transport coal from the local colliery. The stone built quay is still visible with a footpath leading through Hook Wood from New Road just opposite Greenway Close. A tram road was also built. Carts hauled by bullocks were used to transport the coal from colliery to the quay.

In 1795 colliers from Hook, armed with 'oaken bludgeons', travelled to Haverfordwest shouting "One for all", intent on seizing food from a sloop on the quay, but were prevented by the militia. Some of the women attacked Revd Doctor John Philipps, the local magistrate. There was rumoured to be a plan to seize a sloop as it passed Hook Quay and take its cargo of butter. A tender was ordered to accompany the sloop, but its draught was too large for the Cleddau and when the sloop sailed on the tide it had a magistrate and 20 militia on board. It passed Hook without incident.

Pill Road leads to Sprinkle Pill, a tidal inlet. The word pill is common around the Haven and appears to be a term used for a tidal inlet in Pembrokeshire and the West Country with examples in Cornwall such as Pont Pill near Fowey and Pill on the tidal Bristol Avon. The derivation is unclear and may be from the Welsh *pwll* meaning pool.

Houghton

Houghton is a small modern village on the road to Burton from Haverfordwest that has expanded in recent years. There are just a few older houses though next to the school, in Vale Road, was Bishop's Well.

Howelston

Howelston is a farm and caravan park three quarters of a mile south-west of Little Haven, just off the coast road. Fenton describes one of two Iron Age earthwork forts or settlements running up the small valley with the now denuded remains of a round barrow further up the hill.

Hubberston

Hubberston is now a suburb of Milford Haven, but historically is much older than the adjoining town from which it is separated by Hubberston Pill. The name is thought to derive from a 9th century Viking chieftain, Hubba who wintered in the Haven. St David's Church dates from the 15th century, though parts of the fabric are certainly older, with a 13th century font. The tower is tall and the church has undergone a number of restorations.

Hubberston Fort was built in the 1860s as a defensive measure against French invasion. Originally containing a battery of 28 guns, eight were replaced by Moncrief Guns set on carriages so that they were only visible when actually firing. The fort was abandoned after World War I but brought into service again in 1939 as an air raid shelter and US Army base, but is now disused. While it offers views across Gelliswick Bay and the Haven, it is in a dangerous condition due to vandalism and neglect.

To the north of the village on Hubberston Pill are the remains of Pill Priory. Belonging to the Order of Tiron and dedicated to St Budoc and the Blessed Virgin. The Priory was founded in the 12th century. The monks later abandoned their order in favour of the Benedictines. The remains are still clearly visible, though some of the stone has been used in the building of local properties including the Priory Inn.

Sir William Hamilton, had inherited an estate in the area through his first wife, Catherine Barlow daughter of John Barlow of Slebech. He was, with his nephew George Greville, responsible for the development of the town of Milford Haven. Sir William was Ambassador to Naples and took as his second wife Emma Hart. Apparently Greville, son of the Earl of Warwick had taken up with the beautiful Emma but had run into debt and made a bargain with Sir William, whereby Emma was enticed to Naples and was married. The subsequent affair with Nelson is possibly understandable.

Hundleton

Hundleton is an expanding village with a number of small estates one and a half miles west of Pembroke. There are a few older properties including the Calvinistic Methodist and English Presbyterian Chapel built in 1820 and subsequently rebuilt in 1879.

The name is thought to derive from a farm where hounds were kept. A wood south of the village is called Kennel Wood. Today there is just one inn, the new Highgate Inn opposite the sports fields.

A little over a mile south of Hundleton is the Orielton Estate. Now a field Study Centre, the estate came into the hands of the Owen family of Anglesey in 1571, through the marriage of Sir Hugh Owen with Elizabeth Wirriot. The Wirriots traced their history in Pembrokeshire to the 12th century and Elizabeth was a granddaughter of John Philipps of Picton Castle. Various members of the Owen family served as Members of Parliament for Pembroke and were connected through marriage with other county families including the Philipps, Perrots and Laugharnes. Orielton was rebuilt in 1813 by Sir John Owen. He, however, ran out of money after disputed Parliamentary elections and the furniture was sold in 1842 and the estate in 1856. Later the house was reduced in size with five bays being removed.

Jameston

Jameston is a village on the Tenby to Pembroke road. There are some old houses and cottages but the major part of the village is modern.

The Swan Lake Inn dates from the 17th century and there is the Jameston Anglican Mission Chapel dating from 1880, just south of the Inn.

Jeffreyston

Jeffreyston, six miles north-west of Tenby, is an old village which has expanded considerably in recent years. Jeffrey's Tun or Farm was the original name and it is sometimes called Jefferston. At the centre is the parish church of St Jeffrey and St Oswald, a medieval church refurbished in 1867. In the porch is an inscribed slab dating from the 7th or 8th century, indicating the pre-Norman site of the church which was, until the 19th century, set in a raised circular *llan*. The site has been extended for additional grave space. The church cross is a combination of a crude socket stone, a restored base and a modern cross head. St Oswald was the Anglo Saxon King of Northumbria who died in 642 but the dedication to St Jeffrey is unclear.

Jefferston House, otherwise known as the Great House next to the church is believed to be Tudor in origin.

Jefferston Methodist Chapel was established before 1820 but has now been converted to a private dwelling.

The village has the Jeffreyston Inn, situated in the centre at the entrance to the Churchill Park estate.

Coal was mined in the late 18th century but was in decline by the 1830s and ceased in 1867. Jeffreyston had a population of 679 in 1851, but only 49 were coal workers. John Wesley addressed a large congregation of 'honest colliers' at Jeffreyston in 1781.

Johnston

Johnston is a large and expanding village between Haverfordwest and Milford Haven. It is served by a railway station and is now divided between Johnston and North Johnston. There are some attractive older properties and some bungalow estate developments of the 1930s. It was once a mining village, but all signs of that activity have disappeared. There is a small industrial estate in North Johnston.

St Peter's Church was first built in the 13th century with a substantial 15th century rebuild. The tapering tower dates from the early build.

Johnston Hall was the home of a branch of the Butler family in the 17th century, when Lieutenant Colonel Butler was High Sheriff during the English Civil War. The Butlers were landowners in Glamorgan and had arrived in Wales at the time of the Conquest, when the first Butler was a cupbearer to William de Londres. It was later the home of Lord Kensington, an Irish Peerage, who was Father of the House of Commons when he was MP for Haverfordwest during the 18th century. Descended from the Trevor family, he inherited the estates of the Earl of Warwick through his mother. A keen huntsman, it was said that at the age of 86 he could still vault into his saddle without assistance.

Johnston has no less than five licensed premises.

Jordanston

Today Jordanston is a parish with the church of St Cwrda next to Jordanston Hall, the home of the Vaughan family for nearly two hundred years. Situated two and a half miles east of Mathry the parish also contained Llangwarren, the home of the Mathias family for 200 years until 1820. Another local family were the Georges, the ancestors of David Lloyd George.

The parish church is dedicated to St Cwrda, but this is possibly an error as the Welsh translation of Jordanston is Trefwrdan and St Cwrda is a saint more associated with North Wales. The pretty little church has a tower, nave and chancel. The tower was built in 1863 by Col. Sir John James Hamilton and his wife who had inherited Jordanston Hall. The only stained glass window is the East Window which dates from 1949 and was designed by Celtic Studios of Swansea.

In 1896 a stone, being used as a gatepost, was discovered at Llangwarren with Latin and Ogham inscriptions. The inscription read 'TIGERNACI DOBAGNI' in Latin meaning 'Of Tigernacus Dobagnus' and 'DOVAGNI' in Ogham. The stone is now in the garden beneath a shelter. The stone, coupled with the name Llangwarren would appear to indicate the existence of an early Celtic church on this site.

Keeston

The hamlet of Keeston lies north of the Haverfordwest to St David's road, two miles east of Roch. The name is thought to derive from Kessa's Farm. There are a few older properties but most of the housing is modern, though the village green is an attractive feature. The Congregational/United Reform Chapel was built in 1787 and rebuilt in 1856.

West of the chapel is Keeston Castle, an Iron Age fort offering views across to St Bride's Bay. There are three sets of banks and ditches to the central section, with the inner circle measuring 191 feet in diameter and the outer 364 feet. There is an outer much larger enclosure of some 650 feet in diameter and a smaller one to the south, less visible than the other two.

Kilgetty

A large, busy, modern village with local shops and a railway station just under two miles from Saundersfoot.

Kilgetty House was a mansion north of the current village on a site now occupied by Kilgetty Farm. It was the home of Sir Thomas Canon, MP for Haverfordwest and subsequently Haslemere in the early 17th century. It was later the home to the Philipps family of Picton Castle and Sir Richard Philipps, later the first Baron Milford was born there in 1742. There are remains of the gardens and a belvedere connected with the deer park.

The Philipps owned the Kilgetty Colliery which produced high quality anthracite in the early 19th century. Situated at Stepaside, it was reactivated in the 1930s but had ceased production by 1946. There are walls related to the mine in Springburn Close.

Lambston

Lambston is a parish three miles west of Haverfordwest. The church of St Ishmael sits on a cross roads next to Lambston Hall Farm. The church is a simple nave and chancel with western bellcote. Plans for refurbishment were rejected in the 1850s and 1860s but were approved early in the 20th century. There is no village.

Lampeter Velfrey

The name is derived from the Welsh Llanbedr Efelffre meaning the Church of St Peter in the Commote of Efelffre.

Lampeter Velfrey is an attractive village in the east of the county, three miles west of Whitland. According to Giraldus Cambrensis the commote was granted to the Lord Rhys by Henry II and in some accounts the commote had passed by 1186 to his nephews, Hywel and Walter, sons of the princess Nest and uncles to Giraldus. There is a problem with this in that there is no record of a Walter being a son of Nest and her children had died before 1180. Lampeter House is a Victorian building on a medieval site with the early chimney remaining. Farm buildings have been converted into holiday cottages and the house and garden are now used as a concert venue. The house was home to a branch of the Philipps family and there is a memorial tomb in the church. Edward Philipps was Rector of the parish in the late 18th century and was responsible for the Rectory and its gardens. His son Thomas, a failed banker, emigrated to South Africa in 1820, where he founded the settlement of Lampeter, later renamed New Bristol in KwaZulu-Natal. His letters were published in a book in 1960.

North of the church shown on the Ordnance Survey as a motte, is a ring work defensive structure measuring 90 feet in diameter, known as Castell Cyno.

St Peter's is a double aisled church, known to have existed in 1291 though the present structure dates from the 14th-15th century with subsequent refurbishments, the latest in 1997. Unusually for a church south of the Lansker, there is no tower.

The archaeologist Glyn Daniel, who hosted the 1950s television programme *Animal Vegetable Mineral*, was born in the village where his father was the schoolmaster. The Glyn Daniel Laboratory for Archaeogenetics at Cambridge University is named in his honour. He returned to the village and excavated the Parc y Garreg Burial Chamber to the south of the village, west of Bryn Sion Hill. There are clusters of recumbent and standing stones which have been interpreted as two or three burial chambers.

To the west of the village is Llanmill, the site of a major woollen mill dating from 1770, and now a small housing development.

Lamphey

Lamphey is an ancient village originally known as Llantyfai or Church of St Tyfai. Tyfai is thought to have been a nephew of St Teilo. A complication arises in that another dedication for the church is to St Faith and Lewis in 1833, suggesting that the village name was Llanffydd (Church of St Faith). This would appear to be supported by John Leland, the 16th century antiquary who described the village as 'Llanfeith'

The village has expanded significantly in recent years, but the central area around the church is largely unspoilt.

The church of St Tyfai and St Faith is at the heart of the village and its tall 14th -15th century tower dominates. Among the features in the church is one of the finest Norman fonts in the county.

During the 19th century there was no vicarage in Lamphey and at various times the vicar resided at what is now the Dial Inn, Northdown House until, in 1895, Lamphey Hall was bought as a vicarage. It is now a hotel and the present vicarage was built in 1965. The house next to the church was The Venison Inn.

To the north of the village are the ruins of Lamphey Palace. A manor of St David's Cathedral it became the preferred home of the Bishops for hundreds of years. Built and rebuilt, there are features from three periods. The early palace was built probably in the 11th century, rebuilt in the 13th century and then again under Henry de Gower in the 14th century. The palace had four fishponds, a dovecote and deer park. Following the dissolution of the monasteries under Henry VIII, Lamphey was given to Richard Devereux. Walter Devereux was created Earl of Essex in 1572 and the second Earl, Robert, spent his youth at Lamphey before he went to Court and became a favourite of Elizabeth I. He was Lord Lieutenant of Ireland in 1599 but failed to quell a rebellion and made a truce unacceptable to the Queen. He returned to London out of favour and in 1601 attempted a coup. He was convicted of treason and beheaded on Tower Green along with his friend Sir Gilly Meyrick (see Hasguard). The estate was restored to the third Earl who was a leader of the Parliamentary forces in the English Civil War.

The Palace and estate were sold in 1683 to Sir Hugh Owen and it remained in the Owen family until 1822 when it was purchased by Charles Delamotte Matthias. The Matthias family had a long history in Pembrokeshire, but Charles Delamotte Matthias had made his money from West Indian slave plantations. With the Palace in ruins, he built Lamphey Court. Constructed in 1823, it was designed by Charles Fowler. Fowler had won a competition for the design of a new London Bridge but the design was rejected by a committee of MPs. His most famous work is Covent Garden Market. The house was in the Grecian style with a four column Ionic portico. Lamphey Court is now a hotel and spa. The Palace is open to the public 1st April - 31st October (charge).

Timmins in 1895 described the setting: "The graceful character of the architecture, and calm, reposeful situation in this peaceful dell, combine to enhance the peculiar charm that hangs around these venerable ruins. Thanks to the timely care of their present owner, the remaining portions have been preserved from further desecration. Strolling through a ripe old garden, set round with sheltering walls, we proceed to trace such features of the fine old fabric as the hand of Time has spared to us. Passing the refectory, a picturesque building draped in ivy and Virginia-creeper, we are confronted by the tall mass of the banqueting-hall, with its pointed windows and pretty projecting chimney. Hence a winding stair in the thickness of the wall leads to the ruined parapet. Near the east end of the hall stands the chapel, roofless now, and wreathed in luxuriant ivy; one graceful traceried window alone bearing witness to Bishop Vaughan's artistic genius.

Superstitious folk, when approaching these ruins after nightfall, while 'the moping owl doth to the moon complain', may (or may not) have their nerves agreeably thrilled by the apparition of a mysterious white lady, presumably a Devereux, who is said to haunt these historic shades at that witching hour !"

Landshipping

Landshipping is a hamlet on the southern bank of the Eastern Cleddau. The name is derived from 'Long Shippen', meaning a long cow shed.

Landshipping House was built by the Owens of Orielton who were coal agents for the Landshipping Colliery. Known as Big House, it was built in 1750 using stone from an older ruined mansion. The Owens encountered financial problems and the estate was sold in 1856. Despite being purchased by William Owen, a self made businessman and architect, the house was in ruins by 1890. It is now being restored and has been the subject of a number of television programmes including the BBC series *Restoration Home.*

Landshipping Colliery was situated near Landshipping Quay. It suffered a number of disasters. In 1830 five miners died in an explosion while in 1844, at the Garden Pit, some 40 lives were lost when the waters of the Cleddau broke into the mine. A memorial stone was erected in 2002 listing the dead. It is thought that those where the Christian name is given as 'Miner' were women.

The village pub, the Stanley Arms is closed.

Lawrenny

Lawrenny is an attractive village on a promontory between the Daugleddau and Cresswell rivers. A small village, Lawrenny has an active social and sports community. It also has a community shop with broadband service. The derivation of the name is unclear.

St Caradoc's Church is on the outskirts of the village with parts dating back to the 13th century. It is cruciform and has a four storey tower and bellcote.

The Victorian village school was converted into the Millennium Hostel, with 24 beds in five rooms.

Lawrenny Hall was the home of Hugh Barlow, a coal owner, with collieries at Cresswell, and MP for Pembroke. The 18th century house was rebuilt as Lawrenny Castle in the mid 19th century by George Lort Phillips, who inherited the Barlow estate. It is said that Lort-Phillips closed the two village pubs to prevent his staff from drinking and because his wife disapproved of alcohol. John Frederick Lort-Phillips trained racehorses at Lawrenny Farm and met success in 1905 when Kirkland won the Grand National. The family lived at the Castle until it was demolished in 1950. The site is now a picnic area and viewpoint.

During World War II, Lawrenny Quay was a seaplane base. Opened in 1942, Westland Walruses were the first seaplanes based here. Later, Sikorsky Kingfishers and Sae Otter spotter planes were added. The base had only a short life, effectively closing in October 1943. The slipway is the only evidence that a base existed. The Quay is the highest point on the Cleddau that boats can negotiate at low tide. Lawrenny Quay served as a transit dock for the smaller stone and coal barges to transfer their cargoes to larger vessels. Today it has a caravan park, tea room and the Lawrenny Arms, which looks out over the estuary of the Cresswell. There is a pontoon and slipway making the Quay popular with boat owners.

Lawrenny has a counterpart in Tasmania, founded by Edward Lord, a great nephew of Sir William Owen. Born in Pembroke in 1781, he built up a large estate on the River Clyde in Tasmania which he named Lawrenny.

Letterston
The name Letterston is derived from a Flemish settler, Letard Litelking. It is an attractive, large and expanding village ten miles north of Haverfordwest on the A40. The major part of the village lies to the west of the trunk road with shops and imaginative new developments.

The church of St Giles dates back to the founding of the village in the late 11th early 12th century, but now the product of Victorian and 20th century renovations and enlargements. The church was given by Letard's son Ivo to the Knights of St John of Jerusalem who had a preceptory at Slebech. St Giles is equated to the Welsh St Silin. A holy well, Ffynnon Shan Shillin is near the church.

In a field to the north of Station Road is the earthwork of what is thought to have been a Neolithic stone henge, later transformed into one of a number of barrows in the area of the village. To the south of St David's Road a tumulus is marked on the map. This is a ditched mound 60 feet in diameter and six feet high and opinion is divided as to whether this was a barrow or castle mound.

Letterston was a station on the North Pembrokeshire and Fishguard Railway which ran to the east of the village, giving the name to Station

Road. The line closed to passenger traffic in 1937 and to goods in 1949. The track has been removed and the station building is now a private house alongside the loading platform. The Fishguard line runs to the west of the village but there is no station, the nearest being Clarbeston Road.

Liddeston

Liddeston is a small quiet hamlet between Hubberston and Pill Priory. Originally known as Liddens Town the hamlet was the property of Pill Priory and after the Dissolution was owned by the Barlows of Slebech.

Modern development has been of a high quality.

Prior to the building of Milford Haven docks, Haven's Head was used as a small harbour for limestone.

Just outside the village is St Botolph's Mansion. Built for General Richard Le Hunt around 1800, it was formerly in the ownership of the Elliot family. It is thought to occupy the site of a chapel of St Budoc or Buttoc used by the monks of Pill Priory. The property was bought by Amoco for use as a guest house for visiting key staff and as an administration centre. A man staying overnight was awakened by the sound of monks chanting and praying. The house was later converted into luxury apartments.

To the north of Liddestone is the Long Stone Burial Chamber, though the only evidence of this is a six foot stone. North-east of the stone was, according to tithe records, the holy well of St Salmon, though there is no longer any evidence for this.

Little Haven

Little Haven is one of the prettiest villages in Pembrokeshire. Situated in the south-eastern corner of St Bride's Bay, south of Broad Haven, this old fishing village with its colourful cottages is now a popular holiday destination, with a good beach at low tide and a selection of pubs and hotels. The Little Haven beach is narrow, but at low tide it is possible to walk around the headland to Settlands beach which is a wide sandy bay.

Little Haven in the 18th and early 19th century was used for the export of culm of a high quality, though the boats were small, described by Fenton as 'country boats'. Trade was sufficient to justify stationing a customs officer in the village.

Little Haven Lifeboat started in 1882 but closed in 1921 because of lack of coastal traffic, only to reopen is 1967. It was at one time the RNLI's smallest station and since 1989 has operated year round.

Little Haven

Haven Fort Hotel is a converted 19th century fort above the village. It gained wide publicity in April 1977 as the BBC reported "Rosa Granville, who runs the Haven Fort Hotel in Little Haven, was in bed at around 2.30am when she was awoken by strange noise and lights. Looking out of her window, she described seeing an object which looked like an 'upside-down saucer' in the field next to the hotel and two 'faceless humanoid' creatures with pointed heads." This was not the only UFO sighting in the area which for a time was known as the 'Pembrokeshire Triangle'.

Little Newcastle

Little Newcastle, situated two miles north-east of Wolf's Castle is a pretty little village with its church opposite the village green and the Swan Inn. Lewis, in 1833, ascribes its name to the small mound near the church, called 'the castle' which was smaller than the more extensive Castell Pentre, an Iron Age defended enclosure 900 yards north of the village.

The church of St Peter was renovated in the 1840s. It consists of a nave, chancel and western bellcote.

The old school with its clock is now the village hall.

In a field 650 yards from the church is Ffynnon Olden or, as Lewis describes it, Golden Well. Said to have restorative properties for coughs and diseases of the eye, the water level was reputed to rise and fall with the tide in St Bride's Bay nine miles away.

South of the village is Beulah Baptist Chapel. Established in 1808, the 1887 rebuild is in the Art Nouveau style.

Little Newcastle's most infamous son was John Roberts, the son of George Roberts a cattle farmer. John Roberts adopted the name Bartholomew Roberts and is better known as the pirate, Black Bart. Born in 1682, Roberts went to sea at the age of 13. In 1719 he was third mate on the slave ship *Princess* which was taken by pirates off the Gold Coast. The pirate leader was Howell Davis of Milford Haven and Roberts was recruited to the pirate cause. Davis was shot by the Portuguese at Principe and Roberts was elected captain, just six weeks after becoming a pirate. Over the next three years he was to become the most successful pirate in history, capturing 470 vessels. He was killed in a battle with the Royal Navy off the coast of West Africa and with him died the golden age of piracy. There is a plaque commemorating Black Bart in the village.

Llandeloy

Llandeloy is a small village to the north of the Brawdy airfield. There are some interesting older cottages mixed with more modern housing. The village derives its name from the church dedicated to Tylwyf although there is no known saint with this name. Some have suggested that it is a corruption of Teilo. The church dates from the 12th century but was in ruins by 1840. Rebuilt in the 1920s, it is again a redundant church and since 2002 has been in the care of Friends of Friendless Churches. The 1920s rebuild was by John Coates Carter and was greatly influenced by the Arts and Crafts Movement. The church is simple in layout, but has a 'weeping chancel', a feature whereby the chancel is out of line with the nave, reflecting Jesus'inclined head at the crucifixion. There is a bellcote and south transept. The rood screen is beautifully carved with a loft reached by stairs in the north wall which are unsafe.

There is a holy well situated south of the church. Surrounded by a ring of stones it is almost lost in the undergrowth.

Llandruidion

There are two small settlements in Pembrokeshire with this name. The first near Nine Wells is mentioned by Fenton under the name of Llandridion. He reported that a large cromlech had existed in a field adjoining the road. In the early years of St David's, a hospitium (a building offering hospitality to pilgrims) was established here with a prebend attached (i.e. a stipend paid by the cathedral) which was settled on a new dignitary by Bishop Jorwerth in 1224. Signposted off the A487 it is a peaceful collection of farms and cottages. It is a 'No Through Road', but a footpath leads through to the Coastal Path.

The other Llandruidion is a farm on Strumble Head near the hamlet of Trehilyn. Prior to World War I, one of the barns housed a 14 foot water wheel that provided power for a small corn mill. Water came from the pond to the north of the farm. The barns have now been converted into holiday cottages known as Stone Cottages.

Llanfair Nant Gwyn

Situated some one and a half miles south-east of Eglwyswrw, there is no village of Llanfair Nant Gwyn, but the pretty little church of St Mary stands at the entrance to Pantyderi Mansion, formerly the home of the Bowen family. The parish gets its name of St Mary by the White Brook from the white quartz in the local stream. The church was rebuilt in the 1870s and nothing remains of the earlier building save a few tablets. St Mary's has a nave, chancel, bellcote and south porch. Pantyderi now advertises glass manufacturing.

A little over half a mile east, on the B4332, are the Bro Meugan Gardens. St Meugan's Well which was nearby has disappeared, but it was an important Holy Well where fairs were held on Ascension Day and the Monday after St Martin's Day. It was ordered to be destroyed during the 17th century because it was the destination for 'superstitious pilgrimages'.

Llanfair Nant y Gof (See Trecwn)

Llanfyrnach

The village of Llanfyrnach is situated two miles south-east of Crymych, in the valley of the Taf. There are some attractive properties in the village which is dominated by the transport depot of Mansel Davies and Son, which has several depots and garages in the village including the old station yard. Llanfyrnach was on the Whitland and Taf Vale Railway which opened in 1873. The village with its station became a trading centre for the local area. Agricultural produce, silver and lead were sent out and lime brought in. The station was enlarged with a two storey stone building in 1887 and there was a goods yard and two sidings with a loop, the line of which is still visible.

The family of Mansel Davies were originally blacksmiths in the lead mines and expanded into agricultural machinery and then transport. The railway closed in 1963 and the track is now used as an unsightly scrap yard. There is some evidence of the old lead and silver mines in the form of leats used for the water mills, tips and the Cornish engine house which is now a private residence.

The church of St Brynach is situated across the River Taf, west of the present village. St Brynach was believed to be Irish and a chaplain to Brychan, King of what is now Breconshire. After a pilgrimage to Europe, an attempt to assassinate him resulted in his taking refuge in north Pembrokeshire where there are five churches dedicated to him. The present church was established in the precinct of the Norman castle, the motte of which survives across the road from the church. The church was rebuilt in 1842, in the dark grey local stone in a peculiar Elizabethan Gothic style, not helped by the modern white window frames.

Ffynnon Fyrnach, a holy well reputed to have healing properties, exists in the form of a spring. It is to be found in a field a mile and a quarter south of the village behind Rhydmaengwyn.

In a field opposite Tre Henry Farm, three quarters of a mile south-west of the church, are the grass covered footings of Tre Henry chapel. It is believed that this was the original site for the pre-Norman church.

Llangloffan

Llangloffan is a small hamlet half a mile north of Castlemorris and a mile and a half east of Mathry. Named after St Gloffan, an obscure early Welsh saint, there is no sign of a church ever having existed which is strange given the name. The village is however well known for the hymn tune named after it. *Llangloffan* is a Welsh carol or ballad tune, which appeared as a hymn tune in *Llwybrau Moliant* (*The Paths of Praise*), a collection of tunes for use by Baptists edited by Lewis Jones and published in Wrexham in 1872. The Baptist Chapel which was established before 1800 but rebuilt in 1863 is the subject of a lithograph by John Piper in the Tate Collection.

In more recent years Llangloffan has been celebrated for its cheese. Established in 1977 by a former viola player in the Hallé Orchestra, Llangloffan Cheeses which originated at Llangloffan Farm was purchased by the Carmarthen Cheese Company in 2006.

North of the village is Llangloffan Cross, the site according to the 1326 *Black Book of St David's of Maen Gloffan*, a prehistoric stone with possibly a later inscribed cross.

To the west of the hamlet is the Llangloffan Fen National Nature Reserve, home to corncrakes, quails, various species of warblers, otters, water voles and polecats among many other native birds and animals. There is a circular board walk suitable for wheelchairs.

Llangolman

Llangolman is a scattered village two miles east of Maenclochog, on the border with Carmarthenshire. Pont Hywel Bridge over the Eastern Cleddau forms the boundary. There was a medieval bridge here mentioned by George Owen in 1600. It was replaced in 1747 by a twin arched bridge, commemorated by a plaque.

Next to the bridge stands Pont Hywel Corn Mill, now used as The Slate Workshop, producing various items in slate, from house numbers and memorials to clocks and lamp bases.

Named after the Irish St Colman, the village church stands to the south of the main village near the 18th century Llangolman Farm. The church is 12th century in origin, but Victorian restoration has left little of the original.

A mile to the west of Llangolman is Temple Druid House, designed by John Nash who practised in West Wales prior to his time in London where he was responsible for Regent Street, the remodelling of Buckingham House into the Palace and the Brighton Pavilion as well as many other well known buildings. Temple Druid Cottages on the road are contemporary with the house and are thought to be by Nash. Near the entrance to Temple Druid are two standing stones, one on either side of the road, while a third stands south of Prisk Farm.

At Llandilo, between Temple Druid and Llangolman, there is an Independent Chapel, established in 1714 with various rebuilds, the last in 1931. There are the remains of a number of slate quarries in the area.

At Llandilo Isaf, on the road south to Llanycefn from Temple Druid are the remains of the 12th century church of St Teilo, abandoned in the 1850s. The ruined nave and chancel are set in a circular *llan*. Two inscribed pillar stones that were on the site are now in the church at Maenclochog. 250 yards north-west of the ruin is Ffynnon Teilo, St Teilo's Well. A spring set in a rough stone enclosure, the water was said to have healing properties. As with the well at Llandyfân in Carmarthenshire, tradition dictated that the curative properties of the water were enhanced when drunk from a human skull. In the 1890s, a skull was kept at the neighbouring farmhouse for this purpose.

Llangwm

Llangwm (pronounced Langwm) is one of the jewels among Pembrokeshire villages, with its narrow streets filled with colourful, picturesque cottages. Nestling around Llangwm Pill on the Daucleddau, the first written reference to the village was in 1244 when it was called Llandegunnie. The name Llangwm is taken to mean Church in the Valley.

The Church of St Jerome situated in the heart of the village on Butterhill was only so dedicated in 1786 and while the building dates from the 14th century, it underwent a major refurbishment in the 1870s that removed much of the medieval nature of the nave and chancel. The north transept has remained largely intact and contains the monuments of a crusader and his lady, believed to be members of the de la Roche family. The crusader has a thong around his boot that some have likened to a serpent, reflecting the legend of the manner of his death (see Roch). The church has a bellcote in the Welsh style rather than a tower.

Fenton in 1810 comments on the fishing industry, dominated by the oyster which was sold at 6d or 8d per hundred with many being

Llangwm

pickled and sent inland or to Bristol. He remarked on the mountains of oyster shells throughout the 'miserable village' and could not understand why they had not been removed for manure.

The village had a number of hostelries, but the temperance movement forced their closure in the latter part of the 19th century, the last being closed by its teetotal landlord after a haymaker was stabbed during a drinking session. The village now has one pub, the Cottage Inn which was converted from a bakery in 1953. It also boasts a pharmacy and village store together with good sports facilities. Llangwm Pill and Edward's Pill are dry at low tide, but Black Tar slipway provides access to the water for small boats at all states of the tide. Black Tar also has a caravan park. A ferry used to run from Llangwm Ferry on the southern side of the Pill.

Since 1999, Llangwm has staged an annual scarecrow competition on the last week in June and the first week in July.

Llanreath
Llanreath is a village to the west of and now part of Pembroke Dock. There are some attractive Pembrokeshire terraced single storey cottages leading down the hill on Beach Road, with new properties at the bottom above the low cliffs on the Haven. The village backs on to the South Pembrokeshire golf course. The name suggests that there would have been a church in the village, but there is no other evidence for this.

Llanreithan
Llanreithan is parish, four miles north-east of Solva. The church, adjoining Llanreithan House, was rebuilt in 1862 but is no longer in use and falling into ruin. Consisting of a nave, chancel and bellcote, a foundation stone dated 1493 was discovered during renovation but has now been lost. St Reithan has been identified with St Rhidian, an early Welsh saint who converted Brynach Wyddel, King of Gwynedd to Christianity.

Llanreithan Huse is a 16th century house, renovated with a Georgian frontage in the early 19th century.

Llanrhian
Llanrhian is a small village on a cross roads five and a half miles north-east of St David's. There are a number of older buildings around the crossroads, including the parish church of St Rhian, a saint unknown elsewhere, and possibly an abbot. The church was largely

rebuilt in the 1830s apart from the tower which dates from the late 13th century. The 15th century font remains and tradition has it that this came from Jerusalem. It has the coat of arms of Sir Rhys ap Thomas on the side.

Opposite the church is the old school, which is now the village hall, and the old school house.

North of the village, on either side of the road stand Llanrhian Mill House and Llanrhian Mill. The corn mill was working in 1952, but is now a holiday cottage. The village pump stands outside the mill.

Three quarters of a mile west of the village on the road to Square and Compass, are the remains of a Bronze Age burial mound known as Bickney Beacon. Some 75 feet in diameter but less than two feet in height, it was opened by Fenton who found a sealed cist covered by a large capstone.

Around Manor House Farm, in the village, is a group of eight standing stones, but seven are thought to be 19th century in origin, while the eighth is a natural boulder.

Llanstadwell

Llanstadwell is a village west of Neyland, which it once surpassed in importance, running along the north shore of Milford Haven. The name is derived from St Tudwal. The church lies to the east of the village, overlooking the Haven. Although Norman in origin with a 15th century tower and described by Lewis in 1833 as "an ancient structure in good repair", the church was 'vandalised' by the Victorians who in 1876 raised the floor and walls by four feet.

The village has some attractive properties facing the Haven along Church Road, with mainly older properties, apart from a small development of bungalows above Hazelbeach. There is a slipway and pontoon at Hazelbeach, next to the Ferry Boat Inn.

To the west of the village is the giant Dragon Liquefied Natural Gas Terminal, formerly the Gulf Oil Refinery.

Llanteg and Llanteglos

Llanteg and Llanteglos are hamlets either side of the A477 one and three quarter miles from Red Roses. In the parish of Crunwere, Llanteg dates back to the 12th century when it was known as Lann Cronnguern. The name of Lanteg was first used in 1324. Llanteg is to the north of the A477 with new houses in Crunwere Close but there are older farm buildings in East Llanteg Farm. Llanteglos is situated south of the A477 and is largely a modern development of individual dwellings in spacious gardens. Llanteglos House was built in the 1860s and is now a country inn with self-catering lodges.

On the main road, Mountain Chapel, built in 1854 as a Congregational Chapel, was demolished in 2003 and there is now a paved garden within its remaining walls.

Llantood

Llantood is a rural parish in the north of the county, with its church on the A478 Cardigan to Eglwyswrw road, two and a half miles from Eglwyswrw. There is no village. The church is dedicated to St Illtyd and the parish name is derived from the Welsh Llantyd. The church was completely rebuilt in the 1880s to plans by the architect David Davies of Penrhiwllan, south of the former building. St Illtyd's is a standard design with nave, chancel north porch, south vestry and a western bellcote. Preserved in the church is a 14th century stone with an inscribed fleur de lys.

Castell Pen yr Allt, to the east of the church is a mound thought to be of a medieval castle.

Llanunwas (See Solva)

Llanwnda

Llanwnda is a small village, the centre of a parish, in north-west Pembrokeshire. The church of St Gwyndaf was on one of the pilgrim routes to St David's. It is said that on returning from Fishguard, Gwyndaf was thrown from his horse while crossing the brook that forms the parish boundary. He broke his leg and cursed the stream so that no fish would ever live in it.

The little church has overlooked the north coast for 1500 years and is itself overlooked by the Garnwnda burial chamber. Five inscribed stones from the 7th-9th century form part of the outer walls of the church.

There was a major Victorian restoration in 1881, but the church has retained its essential medieval character, with its double bellcote, Sanctus bell, mounting block, leper's squint and the remnants of a narrow staircase.

In the 12th century, one of its clerics was Gerald of Wales while in 1797 the church was ransacked by the French.

A French force of 1400 landed at Carregwastad Head just half a mile north of Llanwnda on 22nd February, 1797 under the command of

Colonel William Tate, an Irish American. The four ships had failed to land at Fishguard as intended, but on landing 800 of the 1400 deserted, looting local villages and farms. Some entered the church, burning bibles and pews for warmth. A maid servant and child hid in the then open rood-loft as the French were creating havoc below. The existence of wine from a recently wrecked Portuguese ship meant that many of the French were drunk. Tate set up his headquarters at Trehowell Farm just under a mile west of Llanwnda. Tradition has it that the French were fooled into thinking that there was a force of grenadiers, by the appearance of local women in their tall hats and red shawls. Local forces were gathered under the command of Lord Cawdor of Stackpole and on the 24th February Tate and his men surrendered unconditionally on Goodwick Sands.

Llanychaer Bridge

Nestling in the Gwaun Valley two and a half miles south-east of Fishguard, little remains of the village of Llanychaer, which was requisitioned by the Ministry of Defence to establish the, now redundant, Royal Navy Armaments Depot, Trecwn in W.W. II. The church of St David, which is 1000 yards south-east of the bridge, was left intact. The church, in a simple style with nave chancel and bellcote, was rebuilt in 1876. Standing in a wooded dell it is said that grass will not grow in the graveyard. In the churchyard is an inscribed stone dating from the 7th-9th centuries. It has a cross inscribed on all four sides. A second stone has now disappeared, but it was inscribed 'Macedeccetus Filius Eorocass'.

The pretty, little village of Llanychaer Bridge has a pub, with a large garden, the Bridgend Inn.

Glandwr Chapel built in 1894 lies between the village and the church. A number of estates dominated the village from the 14th century, including Cilciffeth, Morville, Cilgelynen, and Cronllwyn. All were in ruins by the time of Fenton's visit in 1810.

600 yards to the north of the bridge is Llanllawer church also dedicated to St David. Standing on a hill, it is now redundant, being offered for sale for conversion at the time of writing. The chancel and nave are of a similar width and there is a western bellcote. In the north-east of the churchyard is a holy well, also known as a cursing well, where people tossed pins to bring ill luck on their enemies.

Three quarters of a mile on from Llanllawer church are Dyffryn Fernant gardens, a garden of about six acres including a bog garden, fernery, courtyard, roses, orchard, wildflower meadows, large pond and circular wood.

1400 yards north-east of the bridge is Par y Meirw, the 'Field of the Dead'. There are four standing and two prostrate stones, the tallest being 8ft 9 inches high. Two form the gate post and two more are set into the boundary with the lane. It is suggested that the stones coupled with the name indicate that this was the site of a battle.

Llanycefn (Church on the Ridge)
Llanycefn is a small farming village two and a half miles south-east of Maenclochog. The parish church, dedicated to St Non is set in the centre of a traditional Celtic *llan* and consists of a nave, chancel and bellcote. While there is a clear division between nave and chancel, they are of equal width, though the chancel roof is slightly lower. There was a renovation in 1907. The church is not a listed building and is now redundant.

Llanychllwydog (See Pontfaen)

Llawhaden
Llawhaden, eight miles east of Haverfordwest, is one of the oldest villages in Pembrokeshire. It lies on the Landsker Line and on one of the pilgrim routes to St David's. The name is an anglicized form of Llanhuadain, meaning 'monastic enclosure of the monk Aiden'. Aiden was Irish, a disciple of St David. According to legend, Aiden was charged by David with transporting stone for the building of the church at what is now Lampeter Velfrey. When he came to the ford at the site of what is now Llawhaden Bridge, he said; "What a beautiful place to build a church", which is what he did. St Aidan's Church stands on the banks of the Eastern Cleddau and is well worth the visit. Externally it is unusual in having two towers, a 13th century two storey tower and a 14th century three storey tower adjoining it. External to the church, the towers can be entered via the bell chamber which houses three bells which can be chimed but not rung. The interior has a number of Norman features and there are signs of work during the Tudor and Victorian periods. Nearby Holgan Farm is thought to derive from Heol y Gan or Road of Song, reflecting the pilgrims singing psalms. Holgan Farm now has a fishery with carp, tench and match lakes and an angling school.

On the hill above the church stand the ruins of Llawhaden Castle. The castle was one of three fortified homes owned by the Bishops of

Llawhaden church

St David's, the others being Lamphey and St David's. Only Llawhaden remains as a castle. From the 12th century the Bishops of St David's were Normans who supported the Norman conquest of Wales. They needed castles to defend themselves from Welsh princes. The Lord Rhys, for example, laid siege to Llawhaden and this led to the replacement of the timber castle by the stone building which survives. The building continued through the 13th and 14th centuries and Bishop Thomas Bek, in the late 13th century, established a planned town. It became a borough in 1281 and was licensed to hold markets and fairs. A hospital was established at the western end of the town. King John stayed at the castle in 1210 as a guest of the Bishop and enjoyed the hunting offered locally.

In 1503 Bishop John Margan imprisoned a woman named Tanglost at Llawhaden because of her wickedness. Thomas Wyriott of Orielton, a friend of Tanglost attacked the castle and released her but she continued her wicked ways and was again imprisoned at Llawhaden. Wyriott now petitioned for ecclesiastical absolution and the lady was released but banished from the diocese. She went to Bristol where she conspired with witches to cast a spell on the bishop. They made a wax image and stuck it with pins. The bishop on hearing this sought the help of the Mayor and Corporation of Bristol to help convict the woman who, in fear for her life, denied witchcraft and promised to reform.

After the Dissolution of the Monasteries under Henry VIII the castle was abandoned and became the source of building materials locally. It is said that William Barlow, Bishop of St David's, who had married Agatha, a runaway Abbess of Norfolk, stripped and sold the roofing lead to provide the dowries for his five daughters. The castle is today in the care of Cadw and entry is free. It is open between 10am and 4pm daily. The five storey chapel tower can still be climbed and offers superb views across the Pembrokeshire countryside.

Bishop Bek established the Hospital of St Mary the Virgin, St Thomas the Martyr and St Edward the King in 1287 to care for pilgrims, paupers, aged persons and imbeciles. It was dissolved at the time of the dissolution but the ruins are still visible with an explanatory board at the western entrance to the village.

Owen reported in the 16th century that the borough was in decline.

Llawhaden House in the centre of the village was built in the early 17th century and Cromwell stayed there ahead of the Battle of Colby Moor in August 1645. Sadly the building was destroyed by fire in 2000.

Llawhaden Castle

Llawhaden Mill is a beautiful stone built corn mill, dating from 1765 with its machinery still in place, positioned on the western bank of the Cleddau along from Llawhaden Bridge. The bridge is a three arched structure with cutwater buttresses. There is some dispute as to whether it is medieval or was rebuilt in the 18th century. Giraldus Cambrensis and Archbishop Baldwin crossed the river here in the 12th century by way of a ford.

To the west of Llawhaden is Colby Moor, in 1645, the scene of a battle in the English Civil War in which the Royalists were routed with 150 killed and 700 taken prisoner. The Colby estate was owned by Sir William Hamilton who inherited Colby from his first wife, Catherine Barlow. Sir William passed the estate on to his nephew the Rt Hon. Charles Greville, apparently in exchange for Emma, the Lady Hamilton of Nelson fame. The house was demolished before 1815 and Rees states that a farm had been built on the site.

Three quarters of a mile south-east of Llawhaden is St Kenox, once the home of the Reverend Rees Pritchard, Chancellor of St David's Cathedral and author of the book of religious verse, *The Welsh Candle*. A native of Llandovery where he was vicar before his appointment to the cathedral, which carried with it the living of Llawhaden. He died in 1644.

Llys y Frân

Llys y Frân is a small village two and a half miles north-east of Clarbeston Road. The name translates as Crow's Court. The church of St Meilyr is 12th century with 19th century renovations. Consisting of nave and chancel with a double bellcote, the church is tucked away among trees. St Meilyr was an early Welsh saint, descended from Emyr Llydaw, a Breton missionary. St Meilyr's was a chapel of ease in the Deanery of Rhos before becoming a parish church.

The village of Llys y Frân has little modern development but is adjacent to the Llys y Frân Reservoir and Country Park which offers walking, cycling and fishing. There is a café and visitor centre. The dam, built in 1972, is 100 feet high and controls the flow on the River Syfynwy which supplies much of Pembrokeshire's water, which is extracted near Blackpool Mill. The reservoir has a capacity of 2,310 million gallons.

Loveston

Loveston is a tiny farming village a little over a mile from Jeffreyston with the old village at the end of a No Through Road. The parish church of St Leonard is 15th century with a tapering tall west tower, north and south transepts. It escaped Victorian restoration and so retains many of the original features lost in most Pembrokeshire churches.

Bethel Baptist Chapel was built in 1906 and lies on the B4586, as does the old Loveston School, now a private house.

Loveston was an important medieval freeholding and had a water grist mill and a fulling mill.

Between 1932 and 1937 there was a colliery in the parish. In 1936 seven miners were drowned when water rushed into the mine from old workings.

Ludchurch

Ludchurch (Eglwys Lwyd, the 'Grey Church') is a village in the south-east of the county three and a quarter miles south-east of Narberth. The area has a substratum of high quality of limestone which was used in mantelpieces, taking advantage of its high shine on polishing. There were six limekilns as well as quarries and to the north of the village there are two lakes resulting from quarrying. One lake is now the setting for a caravan park. The church of St Elidyr stands on a hill which Lewis, in 1833, attributes to the land around having been quarried. The church is 13th century with a porch added in the 19th century. The tower is 15th-16th century and the south aisle is 16th century. The interior is mainly Victorian but with Tudor arches. At the edge of the lake below the church are the old lime kilns.

In the churchyard is the grave of Major General John Innes Robinson of the Bengal Lancers. He retired to Hill, Ludchurch. His daughter was Alice Perrin the author of 17 novels and a collection of short stories about Anglo Indian life entitled, *East of Suez*.

To the south of the church is the Ludchurch Cross, with a three step base and socket stone.

At the centre of the present village is Egypt Meadow, at the corner of which are the ruined walls of Egypt Farm. There was once a collection of cottages known as Egypt, the name possibly derived from a gypsy encampment. The old AA sign Egypt is on the wall.

The village today is largely composed of modern bungalows.

Three quarters of a mile south of Ludchurch is Longstone, with Ebenezer Independent Chapel, established in 1848 and rebuilt on a different site in 1862. In a field just south of the hamlet is the Longstone, a standing stone of uncertain age 4ft 6 inches high. On Rosemary Farm is Longstone Camp, an oval banked Iron Age defended enclosure.

On the ridgeway, 1100 yards north-east of Ludchurch church are two Iron Age defended enclosures called Castell Meherin with Parc y Garreg Standing Stone 560 yards to the south-east.

Lydstep

Lydstep is a small village three miles west of Tenby, the name thought to be a corruption of Llys Castell, meaning Castle Court.

Lydstep Palace was a medieval house more properly known as the Place of Arms and was the venue for the manorial court of Manorbier and Penally. It was situated on what is now the golf course. Lydstep Old Palace stands opposite the Lydstep Tavern and is of 14th-15th century origin, built by Henry de Gower, Bishop of St David's between 1328 and 1347. According to tradition, Aircol Llawhir, King of Dyfed, held his Royal Court at this place in the 4th century.

Lydstep Haven is a private beach, backed by a massive caravan park.

Maenclochog

Maenclochog is very much a working village on the B4313 eight miles north of Narberth. The name means 'Stone Bells' and is said to relate to the legend that there were two stones, which when struck sounded like a bell. The stones had already been destroyed before Fenton visited in 1810, in the mistaken belief that they concealed a treasure. Fenton reported that the stones were "about a bowshot from the church to the south-west".

There has been some modern development on the outskirts, but the centre of the village has remained little changed for a hundred years, though it was once a much busier community with no less than seven fairs annually.

At the centre of the village is the church of St Mary which occupies the middle section of a village green. With medieval origins, the church was refurbished in the early 1880s, while the height of the tower was raised in the 1920s with an interesting metal open spire and weather vane. Inside the church are two stones dating from the 5th-6th century, inscribed with the names of two brothers Andagellus and Coimagnus. A third stone was removed from Temple Druid (see Llangolman) to Cenarth in 1743 and appears to be connected with the son of Andagellus. In the 13th century, David de la Roche granted the church of Maenclochog to St Dogmael's Abbey.

There are two chapels in the village, Old Chapel and Tabernacle, while the Tabernacle Sunday School is interesting with a dwelling on the ground floor and the school, now used as a chapel, on the first floor.

The village has a village store, garages and the Globe Inn, though the Castle Hotel has closed. Locals tell that Rocky Marciano, World Heavyweight Boxing Champion 1952-56, was involved in a fight outside the Castle Hotel when he was stationed nearby as a GI in World War II. When the military police arrived, it is said that he floored four of them before being subdued.

To the south of the car park is the site of Maenclochog Castle. Excavations have revealed that there was a defended enclosure with round houses, dating from the Iron Age with a 12th century castle built upon its foundations. The remains are confused by those of an 18th century dry stone pound on the same site.

A branch railway line ran through Maenclochog to Rosebush, with a station to the west of the village, now used as a local bus depot. Beyond the station is Cilmoor Stone, a five foot monolith of uncertain age. South of the village, the railway passed through Castle Tunnel that, in 1943, was used as a target for a prototype of the Barnes-Wallis

Upton

bouncing bomb. Passenger trains had already ceased, but goods trains used the line until 1949.

Just past the 30 mph sign entering the village from the south-west on the Clarbeston Bridge road is St Mary's Well. Tucked away under the hedge on the northern side of the road it is now a spout set in a modern structure, but was originally a spring surrounded by boulders. 650 yards north-east of the church is Galchen Fach Stone, a seven foot standing stone and a small cairn.

One and a half miles south-east of Maenclochog on the Llanycefn road is Penrhos, one of Pembrokeshire's last surviving thatched cottages. This tiny cottage once housed a family of twelve. It was built as a *ty un nos*, a house built in one night, which allowed a house so completed to be built on common land. It was last occupied in 1967 and is now a museum. Opening is by prior appointment by telephoning Scolton Manor Museum on 01437 731328.

Maiden Wells

Maiden Wells is a village, one and a half miles from Pembroke, on an unclassified but busy road. There is a mix of modern housing with some traditional Pembrokeshire single storey terraced cottages.

The name Maiden Wells was first recorded in 1336 as Maydene Welle and is believed to have originated from the local wells being associated with a fertility ritual. Later the wells were used to supply Pembroke with water and while they still exist, they are on private land.

The only place of worship is Gilead Methodist Chapel. There are no shops or inns.

Manorbier

Manorbier is a village on the coast west of Tenby. The name is derived from Maenor Pyr, meaning the estate of Pyr. Pyr is thought to be the 6th century Welsh Saint who founded the religious settlement on Ynys Pyr (Caldey Island). He apparently met his death when he fell into a well while drunk.

According to Giraldus Cambrensis who was born in the castle here, "It is evident, – that Maenor Pyr is the Paradise of all Wales!"

Along with Begelly and Penally, Manorbier was granted to a Norman knight Odo who took the name de Barri from lands he was granted at Baruc (Barry Island) in Glamorgan. Odo built a motte and bailey castle at Manorbier while his son William Fitzodo de Barri built the stone castle. William married Angharad, daughter of Gerald of Windsor and

Manorbier

Nest and one of their sons was Gerald de Barri, better known as Giraldus Cambrensis or Gerald of Wales, cleric and historian and tutor to the future King John. Other sons, Robert and Philip took part in the conquest of Ireland with other issue of Nest. Along with the Fitzgeralds, the Barri's founded dynasties in Ireland. The family remained in possession of Manorbier until the 15th century. The estates were granted by Elizabeth I to Thomas ap Owen and eventually, through marriage, came into the hands of the Philipps family.

The village of Manorbier has changed little and is now a conservation area with some attractive houses and cottages. There is the Castle Inn and a restaurant. Manorbier was the haunt of writers George Bernard Shaw, Virginia Woolf, Walter de la Mare and Siegfried Sassoon.

Manorbier Castle is well preserved, partly due to restoration work carried out by J. R. Cobb in the 19th century who made it habitable. It is open daily 10am-6pm, April to September but may be closed for weddings. The castle commands the beach and was attacked only twice.

Gerald described "The castle called Maenor Pyrr, is excellently defended by towers and outworks, and is situated on the summit of a hill extending on the western side towards the seaport; having on the northern and southern sides a fine fish-pond under the walls, as conspicuous for its grand appearance as for the depth of its water; and a beautiful orchard on the same side enclosed on one part by a vineyard, and on the other by a wood remarkable for the projection of its rocks and the height of its hazel-trees. To the right of the promontory, between the castle and the church, near the site of a very large lake and mill, a rivulet of never-failing water flows through a valley rendered sandy by the violence of the winds".

130 yards north-west of the castle are the remains of the 12th-13th century dovecote which would have housed some 240 birds. The ruined grist mill which lies to the west of the castle is 18th century.

Above the southern cliffs of the beach is the King's Quoit, a Neolithic burial chamber.

The church of St James is large, with a double nave and four storey white tower. Parts date back to the 12th century and there is a 14th century tomb of one of the de Barris and remains of wall paintings. It is one of Betjeman's Best British Churches. Timmins notes: "For quaint picturesqueness, and the singular grouping of its various parts, this curious old church stands unrivalled, even in this land of remarkable churches, combining as it does almost every feature characteristic of such buildings throughout the locality."

In November 1722, four residents of Manorbeer were involved in a murder of some notoriety at the time, which also set a legal precedent. Brothers George and Thomas Merchant were in Tenby at a fair when there was a confrontation with their uncle Thomas Athoe and his son, also Thomas. The quarrel was over an old grudge respecting a share of an estate. A fight erupted in which the Merchants had the advantage and "beat young Athoe". A 'pettifogger' advised old Athoe to seek legal address, but the old man who had in the previous year been mayor of Tenby, refused, saying "we won't take the law but we'll pay them in their own coin". Later in the evening, the Merchants left Tenby, but were followed by the Athoes. At Holloway Bridge the merchants had stopped to water their horses when they heard the Athoes approach. They tried to hide below the bridge but were discovered when their horses splashed the water. The younger Athoe knocked George Merchant off his horse. The older Athoe knocked Thomas off his horse and with cries of "kill the dogs" they beat the brothers with sticks. The elder Athoe then "seized Thomas Merchant in the tenderest part, and so squeezed him in so violent a manner, that human nature could not long have survived the pain; while the younger Athoe treated George Merchant in a similar way, and carried his revenge to such a length, that it is not possible to relate the horrid deed with decency and when he had completed his execrable purpose he called out to his father saying "Now I have done George Merchant's business". A great effusion of blood was the consequence of his barbarity." The young Athoe then bit off George's Nose before strangling him with his handkerchief. The Athoes now left the scene and the Merchants were carried to a local house where George was pronounced dead. The young Athoe fled to Ireland, but was returned. The Athoes were tried at Hereford and found guilty but there was a doubt raised over whether a man could be tried in a county other than where the crime was committed. The Athoes were therefore transferred to London where the King's Bench in Westminster ruled that under an Act in the reign of Henry VIII, "all acts of murder and robberies committed in or around the borders of Wales shall be triable in any county in England". The Athoes were duly executed on 23rd July, 1723, but not before they had attempted to bribe their jailer to allow them to escape.

Manorbier Castle

(The account is taken from the *New and Complete Newgate Calendar or Malefactor's Universal Register 1795*. A fuller account, not sparing the reader's sensitivities is to be found online in the Select Trials for Murders Robberies Rapes Sodomy Coining Frauds and other Trials 1720-1723. http://library.brown.edu/find/Record/b5224703).

Manordeifi

Manordeifi is a parish in North Pembrokeshire, east of Cilgerran with no village of that name. The name derives from Teifi Manor. There are however two parish churches. Manordeifi old church is now in the care of the Friends of Friendless Churches. Dating from the 13th-14th century the church avoided the Victorianisation of the interior, which retains its 18th century box pews, some complete with fireplaces. It is a simple structure with a bellcote, a little over a hundred yards from the River Teifi. The church which it is believed was originally dedicated to St Llawddog, was subsequently dedicated to St David. It was subject to being cut off by flooding and a coracle was kept in the porch to ferry parishioners to high ground. The river no longer floods but the coracle is retained. The church was abandoned in favour of Manordeifi new church in 1899.

Manordeifi new church is situated at Carregwen, 1500 yards south of the old church. Built in 1898, it is a typical Victorian church. Carregwen (translated as White Stone) is a small farming community on a cross roads with a few modern houses and bungalows. To the west is the Cilfowyr Baptist Chapel.

Manorowen

Manorowen is a small village a mile south of Goodwick. The little church of St Mary was largely rebuilt in 1872 with a nave, chancel and a west bellcote.

Manorowen House was built in the 1830s though the Manorowen estate is thought to be medieval in origin. The estate is dissected by both the railway and Fishguard to St David's road. The walled gardens, on the east side of the road, dating from 1750, have been restored and are open to the public.

Marloes

Marloes is an old fishing village with inshore fishermen catching lobster and crab. There was also a harvest of leeches from Marloes Mere and gull eggs from Skomer. Marloes Sands lie to the south with

Musselwick Sands, formerly known as Muggleswick Bay, to the north, while Skomer Island lies off the peninsular to the west.

On the peninsular at the southern end of St Bride's Bay, Marloes today is an attractive village with a good mix of housing including older cottages. There are two inns, the Lobster Pot and the Clock House which stands opposite the Memorial Clock Tower. This was erected in 1904 in memory of the 4th Baron Kensington, a member of the Edwardes family who owned substantial estates locally.

The church of St Peter the Fisherman dates from the 13th century though it was extensively renovated in the 19th century. Unusually for an Anglican church St Peter's has an immersion baptism pool, under a wooden covering. The nave has a barrel roof and the chancel is slightly offset, forming a 'weeping chancel'.

Off Glebe Lane there is evidence of an Iron Age enclosure.

To the west, the tip of the peninsular is a nature reserve which includes a deer park which was designed for deer but never stocked. Martins Haven is still used by small boats.

The derivation of the name is unclear but is thought to derive from the Welsh *Marlais* meaning 'Bare Moor'. It is pronounced locally as Marlas.

Martletwy

Martletwy is an ancient village and a former mining community seven miles south-west of Narberth. The name indicates the grave of a saint, possibly Tywai or Tyfai. Martletwy today is a pleasant rural village. The church of St Marcellus lies to the west of the village. A medieval twin aisled church, though heavily restored in the 19th century leaving just the Norman font and the unusual tomb effigy of a 15th century priest, Sir Phillip, intact. The church was granted to the Knights Hospitallers of Slebech in 1231. The last service was held in January 2011 after which the church was to be partially demolished and managed as a ruin. It is not clear as to which St Marcellus the church was dedicated. To the rear of the church is the old schoolhouse.

Burnett's Hill Chapel lies just under a mile to the south-west of Matletwy. Built in 1812 in cottage style as a Calvinistic Methodist Chapel and opened a year later by the Revd Theophilus Jones, it underwent a rebuild in 1862. Closing in the 1980s, it was taken over by the Friends of Burnett's Hill Chapel and underwent a sensitive renovation in 2008, converting it into a small concert venue holding

100. It was granted Grade II listing for its early character and unusual interior layout.

To the south of the village is Cwm Deri Vineyard. This 25 acre estate has some 3000 vines and has a restaurant.

Mathry

Mathry is a hilltop village in north-west Pembrokeshire bypassed by the St David's to Fishguard road. It is an attractive village with the church on an island in the centre. The Farmers Arms is a traditional village pub, clad in ivy and offering food. The name is shown on Speed's map of 1610 as Merther and is derived from the Welsh *Merthyron* meaning 'martyrs'.

The church of the Holy Martyrs was completely rebuilt in 1869 after the previous building was destroyed in a storm. Designed by Penson, it is a severe building in dark stone. In the graveyard are two early inscribed stones, moved from other parts of the parish. Fenton, in 1811, relates that Mathry was one of the "numerous benefices engrossed by Giraldus; the village and great tithes of this immense parish are the valuable endowment of the golden prebend of St David's, and are now held by Sir Hugh Owen".

In the 14th century, Edward III granted a patent for a weekly market and annual fair to be held in Mathry. The market was abolished, but Fenton records that the fair was still held on Michaelmas Day "when all the servants of the country are hired".

At the time of St Teilo, Cynanwy a Pembrokeshire man and his wife had a child each year but then no children for seven years. They then had septuplets. Knowing that they could not afford to feed such a large family, they decided to drown them in the River Taf. At the river, St Teilo was passing and offered to look after them. He took them to his estate and brought them up as Christians. Every evening, eight fish would appear on a rock in the river to feed Teilo and the seven boys. The estate was subsequently named Llanddowror, because of the children and refers to 'Men of the Water', as they had come from water and had been fed by the water. As adults they came to preach the Gospel in Mathry and were known as the Seven Sainted Men of Mathry. They are said to have been buried in the churchyard. The story is commemorated on the school badge.

In October 1693, Edward Llwyd reported great swarms of locusts in the fields around Mathry, though never seen on the wing.

Merion

Merion is a small hamlet, immediately north of the Castlemartin MOD establishment. There is some modern housing and the 18th century Merion Court, now a working farm.

North-east of the village, and clearly visible from the road to St Twynnells, is Castle Park Enclosure, or the Merion Camp, an Iron Age hill fort. Relatively small but defensively strong with a high bank and a natural slope to the north, it has a commanding view of the surrounding countryside.

Mesur y Dorth

Mesur y Dorth is a hamlet on the A4971 Fishguard to St David's road just north of Croes Goch. The name refers to 'the measure of the loaf', a stone dating from the 7th-9th century set into the wall of Sea View Farm with an incised Latin outline ring cross. The road would have been on the pilgrims' way to St David's and it is believed that the stone marked a point where pilgrims broke bread on their last stop before reaching the shrine.

Middle Mill

Middle Mill is a charming hamlet on the River Solva, one mile inland from Solva.

At the centre is the 16th century corn mill, with its workings intact, but now converted to holiday accommodation. Across the river is Solva Woollen Mill, still in operation. Established in 1907, it produces carpets, some of which were purchased by the Prince of Wales for his Welsh residence Llwynywormod in Carmarthenshire. The mill is open to the public and has a tea room. Below the bridge is a riverside picnic area.

North of the hamlet is Felinganol Baptist Chapel, dating from 1756. It has been rebuilt and refurbished, but retains its total immersion pool.

A little over half a mile north of Middle Mill is Caerforiog, said to be the birthplace of Adam Houghton, Bishop of St David's, 1361-1389 and Lord Chancellor of England under Edward III and Richard II. A farmhouse now occupies the site of the manor house and the adjacent chapel had disappeared as far back as 1866.

Milton

Milton is a village on the A477, eight miles south-west of Narberth and just half a mile from Carew Castle. Divided by the main road, to the north is the attractive old part of the village with the creeper clad Milton Brewery Inn and white washed cottages. The village has grown appreciably in recent years with new developments of bungalows.

To the south of the A477 is Milton House. The Barlow family built a new mansion around 1820 on the site of a house formerly belonging to Upton Castle. The house was transformed with a neo-gothic appearance in 1869. It is now a hotel under the name of Milton Manor. There are no places of worship in the village.

Minwear

Minwear is an ancient parish on the southern bank of the Eastern Cleddau, four and a half miles south-west of Narberth. In the cluster of buildings at Minwear Farm is the little church of St Womar, one of Betjeman's Best British Churches. Dating from the 12th century, this little church is well worth a visit. The parish was granted to the Knights Hospitallers of Slebech some time before 1231, and after the Dissolution of the Monasteries came into the possession of the Barlow family of Slebech. The dedication to St Womar indicates a Flemish influence, as Womar was Abbot of St Peter's in Ghent. To the north of the church a track leads to the site of what is believed to have been a convent, known as the Sisters' House. Here is evidence of a barn, garden and apiary.

The derivation of the name is unclear, but is thought to refer to a weir on the nearby Eastern Cleddau.

Monington

Situated two miles south-west of St Dogmael's, Monington was known in Welsh as Eglwys Wythwr, meaning 'the church of eight men,' as there were eight freeholders in the parish. Apart from a few farms, the parish is dominated by the large gravel pit at Trefigin Quarry.

The church of St Nicholas which is to be found down an unsignposted road, surrounded by trees, was rebuilt in 1860 to a design by the London architect R.J. Withers. There is a stone stile next to the gate and a listed bier house in the graveyard, used to store the cart for carrying coffins. The church has no running water or electricity and is still lit by paraffin lamps. There are murals of angels which are in a good state of preservation. The church has a nave, chancel and western bellcote with the west wall having extra thickness below the bellcote. Church services are still held. The parish is now in the St Dogmael's group.

Monkton

Monkton is a village separated from Pembroke by a stream crossed by Monkton Bridge. Originally the Priory of St Nicholas gave Monkton its name and the church is all that remains intact. There are a number of older buildings of interest around the church and in Church Terrace, but the village has expanded to the west with large housing estates.

The original Norman fortification of Pembroke was at Monkton. In 1098, Arnulf Montgomery gifted the church of St Nicholas within his castle to the Abbey of Seez in Normandy.

Following the Dissolution of the monasteries under Henry VIII, the church gradually fell into decay and it was the efforts of Revd David Bowen, who was vicar for 50 years from 1877, that led to the restoration and the unveiling of the East Window by King Edward VII in 1902. The church has a 12th century nave with a pointed barrel roof, a 14th century chancel, a tower with a south chapel beneath and a north chapel. Inside are a number of rare items, including a 1604 copy of the *Book of Common Prayer*, which survived Cromwell's suppression.

To the west of the church is what is left of the Priory. It is thought that Priory Farm which is a 17th-18th century building has elements of the prior's house. There was also a granary in this area.

St Nicholas' Well is now enclosed, but, situated at the end of The Old Conduit, is thought to have been the water supply for Pembroke Castle.

Morvil/Morfil

Situated seven miles south-east of Fishguard, the parish of Morvil lies between Mynydd Morvil and Mynydd Castlebythe in the western foothills of Preseli Mountain. The ruined church of St John the Baptist stands next to Morvil Farm and is not accessible. The church was rebuilt in the late 19th century to plans by Barker of Hereford. In the churchyard are two early medieval inscribed stones.

Moylgrove

Moylgrove is a village in North Pembrokeshire, three miles south-west of St Dogmael's. Originally called Matilda's Grove, the name gradually evolved to Moylgrove, although the alternate spelling of Moylegrove is used.

There is a mix of housing with some appealing older colour washed cottages. The church of St Andrew lies outside the village on a hill. The small church of 1814 was rebuilt in 1866. A church has however existed on this site from medieval times.

The Nant Ceibwr flows down from Moylgrove to Ceibwr Bay which was used as a port for small ships to bring in culm until 1926. Coastal erosion allied with a fault line has created some spectacular coastal scenery with natural arches.

There were two pubs at Ceibwr in the 19th century as well as seven in the village. All have now closed, as has the village school.

Mullock

Mullock is a hamlet a mile and a half north of Dale. It consists of Old Mullock Farm and some cottages, but in 1485 it is said that Sir Rhys ap Thomas crouched underneath Mullock Bridge to fulfil a prophecy that Henry Tudor would go to the crown over an illustrious Welshman's back. Another version of the story is that Rhys had sworn an oath to Richard III that anyone landing in West Wales would have to ride over his belly and the Bishop of St David's had suggested going under the bridge as a means of abiding by his oath. The old bridge is now bypassed on the B4327.

Mynachlog-ddu

Mynachlog-ddu is a village in north-east Pembrokeshire at the southern side of Mynydd Preseli. Afon Tewgyll, which with Afon Wern forms the Eastern Cleddau, flows through the village. Mynachlog-ddu means The Black Monastic Grange. Black Monks were Benedictines and the Abbey of St Dogmael's was a Bendictine monastery. Bethel Baptist Chapel is situated in the village but St Dogfael's parish church is at Llandre, just over a mile and a half to the south. St Dogfael is also known as St Dogmael. The small church is double aisled with a bellcote.

Around Mynachlog-ddu the hills are scattered with cairns, stone circles and standing stones. Near here the bluestones of Stonehenge were quarried. In Welsh folklore, King Arthur hunted the giant wild boar, the Twrch Trwyth on Mynydd Preseli, but the boar killed two of his sons. Cerrig Meibion Arthur (Stones of Arthur's Sons), two seven foot standing stones, stand north of the cattle grid, one and three quarter miles west of the village.

A little under a mile south of the village is the Gors Fawr Stone Circle, a near perfect circle of 16 stones. There is a lay by and sign on the road. Half the stones are bluestones from Caer Meini and two standing stones nearby appear to frame Carn Menyn to the north.

Nash

Nash is an old parish in Pembrokeshire, straddling the A477, two miles east of Pembroke. There is no village, but there has been some limited development at Upper Nash which has a small terrace of single story cottages. The church of St Mary is situated at Lower Nash Farm, north of the A477 and is an unusual building with nave and chancel of the same width. The interior has been preserved with box pews, a double decker pulpit and a western gallery. There is a bellcote above the western main entrance which has a window above the door. Fenton described the church as ruinous, while Lewis described it as being an "ancient structure, remarkable for the rude simplicity of its architecture".

Buried at Nash is Lewis Watkins. Elected to Parliament in January 1545 for Pembroke Boroughs, before Parliament met he was convicted for the murder of Roger ap Watkin of Llangorse. He was pardoned by the Privy Council and the King, but the widow of Roger pursued the prosecution and the King ordered the Council to devise a method of pacifying the widow "so that the widow may be contented, and yet the law not seem to be impeached". Watkins was dead by February 1548. He retains the dubious distinction of being the only MP elect to have been convicted of murder. Coming from Llangorse, Watkins had been a Yeoman of the Guard and Sergeant at Arms, accompanying the King on his campaign of 1544. He had been appointed Bailiff and Receiver of four lordships in Pembrokeshire and had leased land and tenements at Upton in 1541.

Nevern

Nevern is a small attractive village east of Newport in the north-west of the county. It is set on the confluence of the Afon Nyfer and Afon Gamman. The stone bridge over the Nyfer is 17th century. The village takes its name from the Afon Nyfer.

The church of St Brynach is Norman in origin, but apart from the tower has been extensively renovated. Established as far back as the 6th century as a monastic centre by Brynach, Nevern was an important religious centre. (Details of St Brynach are given in the Llanfyrnach entry.) There are a number of 5th century stones in Latin and Ogham. The Vitalianus Stone is inscribed in Latin 'VITALIANI EMERTO' and in Ogham 'VITILANI' and stands in the churchyard. Some have conjectured that this marked the grave of the 5th century British warlord Vortigern, under his family name of Vitalinus. The Maglocunus Stone inscribed in Latin 'MAGLOCUNI FILI CLUTORI' and in Ogham 'MAGLICUNAS MAQI CLUTAR' is set into the wall of the Henllys Chapel in the church, as is a 10th century braided cross. In the churchyard is the 10th century Nevern Cross or St Brynach's Cross.

Outside the churchyard is a mounting block, built to assist horse riders mount their steeds in the days when many went to church on horseback.

St Brynach's Day is 7th March and it was said that the cuckoo always appeared at Nevern on this day. The tradition was that the priest would not begin mass until the cuckoo arrived and perched on St Brynach's Cross and sang. One year storms delayed the bird until dusk, the priest had delayed mass and when the exhausted bird finally arrived he perched on the cross, sang the first two notes and then dropped dead, but mass could at last commence. As the Tudor historian George Owen commented, "This religious tale you may either believe or not without peril of damnation".

A yew tree in the churchyard 'weeps' red resin at certain times of the year, and attracts both Christians and Pagans for whom it is the embodiment of the great goddess mother. A recessed orifice in the bark is symbolic of female genitalia.

Nevern Chapel was built in the early 19th century, but converted into a school and is now the village hall.

On a hill surrounded by woodland to the north of the church stood Nevern Castle, Castell Nanhyfer. A motte and bailey castle was constructed on the site of an Iron Age promontory fort by the Fitzmartins in the early part of the 12th century. It was seized by the Gruffydd ap Tewdwr in 1136, but later regained by William Fitzmartin through his marriage to a daughter of the Lord Rhys, Gruffydd's son. He in turn was turned out by the Lord Rhys who was in due course imprisoned there by his sons. He died there in 1195 after which the castle was dismantled. Nevern was one of the earliest Welsh stone castles. The ruins are now in the ownership of Nevern Community Council. There are way marked trails, information boards and a picnic area.

For such a small village the Trewern Arms is a large inn with a restaurant and accommodation.

On a path, not shown on the Ordnance Survey map, leading from the point of the sharp bend on the road leading to the castle, is a pilgrim's cross cut in relief in the rock. This was on the old Pilgrims' Way to St David's. A scheduled ancient monument, it is thought to be unique in Wales.

Within the parish, a mile and a half to the north-west is Gethsemane, a hamlet with the now converted Calvinistic Methodist Chapel and graveyard which appears to be still in use. On some maps, the hamlet is shown as Tredrissi. Three quarters of a mile north-east is

Trellyffaint Farm, or Toad Town Farm, so named because according to Giraldus "a young man suffered as violent a persecution from toads, as if the reptiles of the whole province had come to him by agreement: and though destroyed by his nurses and friends, they increased again on all sides in infinite numbers, like Hydras' heads; his attendants being tired out he was drawn up, in a kind of bag, into a high tree stripped of its leaves and shred; nor was he safe there from his venomous enemies, for they crept up the tree in great numbers, and consumed him to the very bones". In 1815 a marble toad was attached to a chimney, though it was subsequently reported to have been removed to a house in Haverfordwest.

One notorious son of Nevern was William Owen, born to a wealthy local farmer in 1717. Educated at Cardigan, Owen went to sea at the age of 14. At the age of 16 his father purchased a boat for him and for a while he traded honestly. He then took to smuggling. His life for the next 14 years was a series of adventures. His ship was seized by customs in the Isle of Man and Owen joined the *Terrible*, a well armed smuggler sailing in the West Indies. He led the crew against two Spanish ships. He was welcomed as a hero in Barbados and while not indulging in drink or swearing, "gave himself up to women, embracing all opportunities", with babies "of all colours" the result. Owen was captured by a British Man of War, but the captain took Owen on as a midshipman. After two years he returned to Cardigan a wealthy man, in 1739. He acquired a vessel and returned to smuggling with some success, until in 1741 his ship was attacked by corn rioters in Cardigan. He drove off the rioters by shooting and injuring their leader. He now joined his friend Thomas Parry, an Aberystwyth attorney, in an attack on the Aber-mad mansion of Thomas Johnes, High Sheriff of Cardiganshire. There was a pitched battle which ended when Owen blew up a wagonload of gunpowder under the mansion's balcony.

Owen returned to smuggling but in 1844 was met by a Customs collector at Cardigan, accompanied by twenty assistants composed of four Spanish prisoners of war, two convicts, a tide-officer and "supernumery catch poles and informers". Owen and his crew killed two Spaniards and two Welshmen, one of whom was the Customs officer. Owen escaped to the Isle of Man but was eventually arrested and tried at Hereford. Owen defended himself and was acquitted on the charge of murder but found guilty of manslaughter and released. He became master of a privateer, the *Admiral* Blake but he and the

crew fell victims to an illness off the Barbary Coast. He returned to
Cardiganshire and in circumstances which are not entirely clear he
murdered James Lilly, with whom he was running from a hue and cry.
Owen was convicted of murder and hanged at Carmarthen on 2nd
May, 1747 at the age of 30.

New Inn
Situated at the southern foot of Mynydd Preseli midway between
Cardigan and Haverfordwest, on a cross roads off the B4313 and the
B4329, Cross Inn was a coaching inn, now closed. Malkin told of a
traveller who publicly claimed to have been served goose at the New
Inn, but cautioned that he could get nothing to eat.

New Hedges
New Hedges is a village a little over a mile north of Tenby on the A478
Narberth road, though the village is largely bypassed. There are a
number of large caravan parks, though the village has more of a
suburban feel with new housing. There is a small supermarket and
old school. The church of St Anne's is to the south of the village on the
main road and was built as a Mission Church or 'Tin Tabernacle', from
corrugated iron and painted blue and white. The church has been
recently restored and there is attractive wrought iron work in the
railings leading down from the road.

New Moat
New Moat is a small village in central Pembrokeshire three and a
quarter miles north-east of Clarbeston Road. The term moat was used
in the area as an alternative to castle, and New Moat was used to
distinguish it from Henry's Moat nearby which, according to Fenton,
was Castell Hendref or Old Town Castle. It is thought both were
established as Flemish settlements.

There are some attractive older properties and limited modern
development. The village takes its name from the motte and bailey
castle, the motte of which stands in a field opposite the entrance to
Beech Close. 130 feet across and 16 feet high, the motte has a further
mound on top, the origins of which are unclear. The line of the bailey
is defined except to the north-east.

The village was the home of the Scourfield family from the reign of
Edward I. It is said that the name was bestowed on the family by King
John, in 1210, during his stay at Llawhaden. The King was so

impressed with a greyhound owned by the forester that when presented with the hound he named Scour the Field, he bestowed the name on the forester and his crest was a greyhound courant. Mote House, their residence, was rebuilt in 1830 but demolished in 1926. The family, who had moved to Robeston in the 18th century, had taken up residence at Williamston, following the marriage of the heiress into the Phillips family (later changing the spelling to Philipps, though an heiress subsequently married into the Philipps family and changed their name to Scourfield!) and may never have occupied the house. The entrance was to the south of the church and the lodge has been modernised. The drive crossed the fishpond before meandering through a plantation to the house.

St Nicholas Church retains its medieval tower but was extensively refurbished in the 1880s and more recently with the aid of a Heritage Lottery Fund grant. Inside there is the altar tomb of William Scourfield who died in 1621.

Newgale, Pembrokeshire
Newgale is a hamlet on the west coast, south of St David's. There is a good sandy Blue Flag beach, stretching for nearly three miles, except at high tide, with the community at the northern end and climbing Newgale Hill. There is a beach shop and the Duke of Edinburgh tavern. It is regarded as one of the best surfing beaches in the county. Camp and caravan sites lie to the south.

Newton Mountain
Newton Mountain is a small community of mainly modern bungalows, west of Hill Mountain on the road from Haverfordwest to Burton. Indeed the signposts read Hill Mountain. The most interesting feature is the Listed Port Lion Mission Chapel situated behind bungalows at the southern end of New Wells Road. It is constructed of corrugated iron and painted black.

Newton North (See Bluestone)

Nine Wells
Nine Wells is a hamlet on the A487 one mile west of Solva. There are just a few farm buildings and the Nine Wells Caravan and Camping site. The hamlet takes its name from the nine wells locally, one of which is clearly visible south of the road just west of the caravan park entrance.

It is a stone basin enclosed in a six foot six inch high roofed chamber. North of the road was an army camp and the St David's airfield.

Nolton and Nolton Haven
Nolton is a lovely old village inland from Nolton Haven which lies south of Newgale Sands. The name is thought to be derived from 'old town'. The area was known for its purplish stone, reputed to be near the quality of Portland Stone. The Haven was used for the export of culm, which was produced from the anthracite which was also found locally.

The church of St Madoc is a simple nave and chancel with bellcote structure, nestled below the road level. Inside Fenton praised its neatness and decency, which the church retains to this day. The Glebe House, opposite the church, was the Rectory which Fenton dates from the 14th century and is one of the oldest continuously used rectories in Wales, though it was extended in the 19th century, with a new facia and has recently been refurbished as holiday accommodation. Next to the church is the hall, built around 1810 as a school by the Reverend Moses Grant.

Fenton suggests that to the north of the church there was once a manor house.

At Nolton Haven there is a good sandy beach with the Mariners Inn and the United Reform Chapel. There is a caravan park up further up the valley and a slipway for launching small boats.

Pelcomb Cross and Pelcomb Bridge
Two small communities on the A487 lie within two and a half miles of the centre of Haverfordwest, on the way to St David's. Pelcomb Bridge has the Rising Sun while Pelcomb Cross has the Pelcomb Inn.

Penally
Penally is an ancient village to the west of Tenby. The main coastal road which bypasses the village is lined with caravan parks, taking advantage of the good sandy beach which extends from Tenby's South Beach.

The village itself has narrow streets and picturesque old buildings. Its name is thought to derive from *Pengelli*, meaning 'Head of a Grove'.

It is reputed to have been the birthplace of St Teilo. Legend has it that on the death of St Teilo, at his monastery at what is now Llandeilo in Carmarthenshire, clerics from Penally, Llandeilo and Llandaff, where he had been bishop, all laid claim to his body. Unable to agree, they prayed for guidance and lo and behold, the next morning there were three bodies of St Teilo, one for each. It is likely that the story came about through the efforts of Llandaff Cathedral in the 12th century to rewrite its history, as there is no earlier evidence of Teilo having a connection with Llandaff.

The church is dedicated to St Nicholas and St Teilo, though the dedication to Teilo did not occur until the 19th century. The church stands on the village green, and dates from the 13th-14th century though the Celtic Crosses now in the church indicate that this was a site of some importance, probably a Celtic monastery. There is evidence of wall paintings, but the renovation of 1851 covered these. There are a pair of squints. The tower is slender and two piscinas suggest that it may have been the practice locally to enter via the south door but leave through the tower.

The Penally Cross, now in the north transept is particularly interesting as it appears to combine Celtic and Northumbrian traditional carvings.

Above the church on the road to Penally Abbey Hotel is St Daniel's Well, a medieval well with stone surround. Opposite is the site of St Deiniol's Chapel, described by Fenton as a Chantry Chapel. (St Daniel's Well is the name given by CADW, It appears elsewhere as St Deiniol.) An ancient manuscript described how "a certain woman from the district of Caerw (Carew), in the diocese of Mynyw, was so swollen beyond measure that she could find no relief by any advice of physicians. At last, coming to the church of St Deniol, and afterwards to the aforementioned well, and imploring the Saint's help, she drank of that water so as to regain health and before leaving came to the entrance of the Church, and cast forth from her mouth, while many stood by and observed, three horrible worms, each with four feet, and the woman was made whole from that very hour."

The Cross Inn is situated on Strawberry Hill near the church.

The Penally Abbey Country House Hotel was built in the 1840s as Penally House. It was the first house in Pembrokeshire to be lit by electricity and its owner, Clement Williams Esq, mayor of Tenby, also installed electric lighting in the church.

On the cliffs south-west of the village are a series of practice trenches from World War I. There are two firing trenches in the zig-zag pattern, to help prevent the spread of blast, linked by communication trenches. They cover a considerable area and in parts were dug into the bedrock. There is a rifle range south of Penally station. Originally established in the 1850s, it was used in World War II for mortar and grenade practice.

Just past the 40 mph sign entering Penally from Tenby, the road crosses Holloway Bridge, the scene of the murder of Edward Merchant in 1722, as described under Manorbier.

Hoyle's Mouth Cave is a natural limestone cave that has been in use since the Stone Age. Situated north of the village, off Trefloyne Lane, the cave is now home to colonies of Lesser Horseshoe and Pipistrelle bats and should not be entered. A local legend said that the cave was connected to a cave beneath Pembroke Castle.

Penbedw/Llanfiangel Penbedw
The old parish of Llanfiangel Penbedw is located three quarters of a mile north of Boncath. The church, built on a Celtic *llan* is derelict and is found at the end of the lane leading to Penbedw Farm. *Penbedw* is Welsh for 'Head of Birch'. The church dedicated to St Michael was abandoned in 1970 and from signs on the floor is now used as a shelter for farm animals. The font is in pieces. The church, which was rebuilt in 1869, has a nave chancel and tower with a gable roof. Surrounded by trees this church presents a sad but peaceful aspect.

The route of the Whitland to Cardigan Railway is to the east of the church.

Pen-Ffordd
Pen-Ffordd is a hamlet in the parish of Bletherston and lies three quarters of a mile north-east of Bletherston village. The name means end or head of the road or way, and the main road through Pen-Ffordd is Longridge Road. There is a mixture of housing in essentially a farming community. At its centre is the Calvinistic Methodist Chapel established in 1861 and restored in 1913.

Pennar/Pennar Park
Situated south-west of Pembroke Dock, Pennar today is a large housing estate, partly facing the South Pembrokeshire Golf Course. Pennar Park is a new development of houses and apartment blocks at the western end of Military Road overlooking the haven and Pennar Mouth at the entrance to the Pembroke River.

Pennar was part of the estate of Hywel Dda, and was granted to his grandson Jestyn in 948. In 1183 it passed through marriage to the Perrot family. In 1363 it was known as Estpenr and the name Pennar had become established by the 16th century when it was described by George Owen as "groweth one of the best Oysters of all Milford being a bigg and sweet oyster". The estate eventually passed through marriage to Sir William Owen of Orielton. In the 19th century Pennar was occupied by workers from the Pembroke Naval Dockyard. Housing was not up to modern standards and most was demolished in the 1950s when the new council estate was built. The South Pembrokeshire Golf Course occupies land formerly used by the Admiralty and Ministry of Defence which had been acquired from Sir John Owen in 1822.

Pennar Park was the site from 1875 of the Royal Navy's Torpedo stores. After World War II it was converted into Pennar Park Holiday Camp before the modern development of apartments.

Pentlepoir

Pentlepoir is a village on the A478 one and a half miles north-west of Saundersfoot. Stretching along the main road, the village has extended into Wooden and Hill. And there are housing estates on both sides of the main road. There is a mixture of modern developments and a small number of older houses, together with two service stations and numerous caravan parks. There is the Woodridge Inn Hotel and the Dragon Palace.

Pen y Bryn

Pen y Bryn (Brow of the Hill) is a village in the north of the county, on the A478. It is the first village in Pembrokeshire travelling south from Cardigan. As the name suggests it is on the breast of a hill and there is a crossroads with the road to Cilgerran to the east and Nevern to the west.

It was a ribbon development with new housing built along the side routes. The Pen y Bryn Arms sits on the cross. Pen y Bryn Welsh Baptist Chapel was established in 1819 and rebuilt in 1869.

Penrieth /Penrhydd

Also known as Penrith, this was a parish with a church one and a quarter miles south-east of Boncath. The parish took in the Frenni Fawr mountain and there was a chapel of ease at Castellan. The chapel was in ruins in 1833 and situated on the west of Frenni Fawr where Castellan Farm is now. The church of St Cristiolus is situated in woodland next to Dolalau Isaf Farm and is derelict. The translation of Penrhydd is 'Free End'.

Pleasant Valley

Situated between Saundersfoot and Wiseman's Bridge, Pleasant Valley is a ribbon development with caravan parks largely occupying one side of the road and housing mixed with caravan parks on the other. Stepaside Methodist Church was built in 1893.

Pontfaen

Pontfaen is situated in the beautiful Gwaun Valley, four miles to the east of Fishguard. A small community with Cwm Gwaun situated on the opposite side of the river. The name Pontfaen means 'cow bridge', but may derive from the Gwaun river.

Pontfaen House is a 17th century building described by Lewis in 1833 as a handsome mansion. Formerly in the ownership of the Laugharne family the estate was said to offer some of the best grouse shooting in Pembrokeshire.

St Brynach's Church was founded by St Brynach in the 6th century. It is to be found in the grounds of Pontfaen House and is open to visitors in the summer months. The condition of the church deteriorated in the 17th century to such an extent that in 1860 it was in ruins. Pontfaen House changed hands and Percy Arden the new owner undertook a major restoration and built a vicarage. A further restoration took place in 1987.

The church is simple with a nave, chancel and bellcote. The porch was a 19th century addition. There is a small side chapel connected by a hagioscope or squint. Inside there is a wall painting, a copy of *The Tabernacle of the Madonna of the Stars* by Fra Angelico, made by R. Cipriani (Florence) in 1902. In the churchyard which is the typical circular shape of a pre-Norman Celtic *llan* are two pillars possibly dating from the 6th century, though inscribed with 9th century crosses.

The Dyffryn Arms is a popular local hostelry which has been in the same family since 1840.

The local community have never accepted the change from the Julian Calendar and still celebrate New Year on 13th January.

To the east of the village is Castell Pengegin, one of three Iron Age hill forts in the woodland north of the village.

A little over half a mile south-west of Pontfaen is the Gwaun Valley Brewery. Situated in an old granary at Kilkiffeth Farm, it is open seven days a week, 10am-6pm.

Three quarters of a mile west of Pontfaen, on the northern side of the river, is the little church of St David in the parish of

Llanychlwydog. Now converted into a private dwelling with the font placed outside, under the bellcote. There are four pillar stones in the churchyard with inscribed crosses. Llanychlwydog County Primary School is located on the banks of the Gwaun, three quarters of a mile east of Pontfaen. The name Llanychllwydog is difficult. The literal meaning is 'church of the grey ox harrow'. In the story below however the name is given as Llanferch Llawddog, meaning the 'Daughter church of St Llawddog'.

Wirt Sykes gives the following account of a spectral funeral in his book *British Goblins*: "Morris Griffith was once schoolmaster in the parish of Pontfaen, in Pembrokeshire, but subsequently became a Baptist preacher of the Gospel. He tells this story: "As I was coming from a place called Tre-Davydd, and was come to the top of the hill, I saw a great light down in the valley, which I wondered at; for I could not imagine what it meant. But it came to my mind that it was a light before a burying, though I never could believe before that there was such a thing. The light which I saw then was a very red light, and it stood still for about a quarter of an hour in the way which went towards Llanferch-Llawddog church. I made haste to the other side of the hill, that I might see it farther; and from thence I saw it go along to the churchyard, where it stood still for a little time and entered into the church. I remained waiting to see it come out, and it was not long before it came out, and went to a certain part of the churchyard, where it stood a little time, and then vanished out of my sight. A few days afterwards, being in school with the children about noon, I heard a great noise overhead, as if the top of the house was coming down. I ran out to see the garret, and there was nothing amiss. A few days afterwards, Mr. Higgon of Pontfaen's son died. When the carpenter came to fetch the boards to make the coffin, (which were in the garret), he made exactly such a stir, in handling the boards in the garret, as was made before by some spirit, who foreknew the death that was soon to come to pass. In carrying the body to the grave, the burying stood where the light had stood for about a quarter of an hour, because there was some water crossing the way, and the people could not go over it without wetting their feet, therefore they were obliged to wait till those that had boots helped them over. The child was buried in that very spot of ground in the churchyard, where I saw the light stop after it came out of the church. This is what I can boldly testify, having seen and heard what I relate – a thing which before I could not believe."

Portfield Gate
Portfield Gate is a hamlet two miles west of Haverfordwest on the B4341. A ribbon development with a mix of housing, including some attractive older Pembrokeshire cottages.

Porthclais
Porthclais is a harbour south-west of St David's. The harbour wall is believed to have been built by the Romans. It was the port for St David's, from the 12th century with small boats bringing in coal and timber. There are two pairs of well preserved lime kilns. Porthclais was mentioned in the *Mabinogion*, the 11th century book of Welsh tales as the landing place of the Twrch Trwyth, a legendary wild boar pursued by King Arthur. Arthur's sons were killed in the chase and are said to be buried at the Cerrig Meibion Arthur near Mynachlog-ddu. It is thought that St Patrick sailed for Ireland from here. He had been taken from Wales as a slave, escaped but was commanded in a dream to return, to convert the Irish to Christianity.

To the east of Porthclais is St Non's Bay. St Non was the mother of St David and the ruins of the chapel on the headland mark the place of St David's birth. The chapel is built north-south, possibly due to the terrain. It fell into disuse after the Reformation and became a private dwelling for a time. There is a modern shrine with a statue of St Non. St Non's well, 40 yards north-east of the chapel, was said to have come into being at the time of St David's birth which, according to legend, was in the middle of a thunderstorm. David's father was Sant, King of Ceredigion. St Non is commemorated in churches at the villages of Llannon in Ceredigion and Carmarthenshire and at Pelynt in Cornwall where there is St Nonna's Well.

Porthclais is still in use today for small fishing boats and pleasure craft. There is a caravan park at Porthclais Farm.

Porthgain
Porthgain (Fair Port), situated on the north coast near Llanrhian, is today a picturesque harbour village, popular with tourists. It was however a centre of industry into the 20th century, with the remains of the brickworks alongside the harbour. The brickworks were secondary to the main export of Porthgain which was slate and crushed stone for road building from the nearby coastal quarries. A tunnel and a series of tramways transported the stone which was exported on the purpose built 350 ton coasters. The bricks were

made to build the hoppers and were subsequently exported to Llanelli and Dublin. There was a crushing plant above the harbour which fed into the hoppers which today are listed buildings. The trade ended in 1931.

The slate quarrying industry at Porthgain was developed by George Le Hunte of Artramont in County Wexford from 1837. The family owned property in the parishes of Llanrhian, St David's, Henry's Moat, Newport, Nevern, Llandissilio West, Llangolman, Llandilo and Maenclochog as far back as the 17th century. George's son Sir George Ruthven Le Hunte, born at Porthgain in 1852, was to become Governor of South Australia from 1903 until 1909.

The pretty terraced cottages that line the road to the harbour were built for the workforce. There were more to the north-west above the industrial complex but these are now in ruins. The roofs of the cottages nearest the harbour are covered in mortar as the local slate is too soft to survive the Pembrokeshire weather.

There are the remains of a lime kiln near the harbour. Lime burning was the first industry of the village. Limestone and coal were brought in and lime produced to improve the quality of the acid-rich local soil. It was also used in mortar and in lime washing the houses.

The small white cottage at the entrance to the harbour was the harbour pilot's.

The Sloop Inn dates from 1743 and originally stood at the side of the harbour before it was filled in to create the road.

Porthstinian/ St Justinians

To the west of St David's is the harbour of Porthstinian with the ruined chapel of St Justinian.

St Justinian, a Breton sometimes referred to as St Stinian, established a religious community on nearby Ramsey Island in the 6th century. Such was the strict discipline he imposed that his monks rebelled and beheaded him, whereupon he picked up his severed head and walked across Ramsey Sound to St Justinians, where he was buried. His remains are said to be in a casket in St David's Cathedral. The ruined chapel dates from the 16th century but there is evidence of a much earlier building on the site. The chapel was a place of pilgrimage, with donations passed to the cathedral. The nearby St Justinian's Well now supplies a local bungalow.

Porthstinian is home to the St David's Lifeboat Station. There is a caravan park but the small beach is unsuitable for bathing.

According to tradition, during the English Civil War, followers of Cromwell carried off a bell from St David's Cathedral but the ship used to transport it sank off Porthstinian. It is said that the sound of the bell can be heard from its watery grave as it tolls whenever a storm is rising.

Princes Gate

Princes Gate, named after a tollgate on the turnpike road, is a hamlet on the crossroads of the B4314 and B4315, two miles south-east of Narberth. In recent years there has been development to the west of the cross. To the east is the pretty little listed mission church of 1900. Princes Gate Spring Water is produced locally.

Port Lion

Port Lion is a ribbon development on a side road leading down to Llangwm Ferry Pill. It is a no through road. Housing is modern.

Puncheston

Puncheston is a working agricultural village five and a half miles south-east of Fishguard. The name Puncheston is thought to derive from Pontchardon in Normandy though an alternative explanation is that it was named after Pointz, who built Pointz Castle near Brawdy. Pointz is pronounced 'punches'.

There are some attractive older houses and cottages with more modern development and the school is located on the road to Trecwn. The school was built in 1953 on the site of a former US Army base where according to locals Rocky Marciano was stationed for a time in World War II.

The church of St Mary is a simple structure with a single aisle and bellcote. The nave and chancel are the same width and the church has no chancel arch. It is first mentioned in 1291, though a Celtic church may have existed on the same ground. The village has Smyrna Baptist Chapel and Bethel Methodist Chapel.

Castell Mael, which gives the village its Welsh name of Cas-mael, is situated above the Afon Anghof behind the farm buildings in the centre of the village. Its origins are unknown and it is described as a defended enclosure. The origin of the name Mael is uncertain and may refer to a stone with Latin inscription CUNISCUS FILIUS NEMAGLUS which is recorded in the British Museum, but is now lost.

Just under 600 yards north of the church is an eight foot standing stone known as Carreg Coitan Arthur. It is situated in the hedge of a field just north of Awel y Coed house on the opposite side of the road. Parc Maen Llwyd Standing Stone is over eight foot and stands in a garden at the rear of a house in Park Avenue opposite the school.

A little over a mile west-north-west of the village is the well outlined Summerton Camp, an Iron Age double ring enclosure.

Puncheston was, until 1949, on a branch railway line to Fishguard. The line ran to the east of the village and the station lay to the north-east where Station View is one of the few signs of its existence.

The village has the Drovers Arms. Puncheston was on the drovers' route and they would leave the animals to graze on Puncheston Common.

The vicar of Puncheston, William Gambold published *A Compendious Welsh Grammar* in 1727. His son John was a contemporary and friend of Charles Wesley, but became a bishop of the Unitas Fratrum in the Moravian church.

Pwllcrochan

Sandwiched between Pembroke Power Station and the Chevron oil refinery on the south side of the Haven, three miles west of Pembroke Dock, all that is left of Pwllcrochan is the old 1861 school and the church of St Mary. Without a congregation, the pretty church closed in 1982 and has been taken over by the oil refinery as an educational centre, ensuring its preservation. The church was rebuilt in 1342 by Rudolph Benegar, its rector, and an engraved stone records this event. The church has a nave, lime washed chancel, north transept and a tower with an octagonal spire on the southern side of the nave. There was a refurbishment in 1865. The interior furniture has been removed, some to Rhoscrowther church. The churchyard was the site of a skirmish between Royalist and Parliamentary forces in 1648.

Pwllgwaelod

Pwllgwaelod is a beach with a café, a few houses and a pub, the Old Sailor, at the south-western end of Dinas Island. The name means 'Bottom Pool'. There is a good beach and slipway for boats together with a large car park. To the north of the beach is the site of an Iron Age promontory fort, with a single rampart across the neck of the promontory.

Redberth

Redberth, now by-passed by the A477, is three miles west of Saundersfoot. The village has grown in recent years but there are some appealing cottages around the church of St Mary. The church was reported to be in a ruinous condition and undergoing complete repair by Lewis in 1833. It has a small west tower with the porch below, a nave and chancel. Opposite the church is the old school with its bellcote, now a private house.

Reynalton

Reynalton, four miles south-west of Narberth, is thought to have been founded by Flemish settlers following the Norman Conquest. The name is thought to derive from 'Reginald's Farm'. Lewis, in 1833, recorded that a number of cottages had the round chimneys typical of Flemish properties. He also reported that the village was in decay. Today the village has expanded with new individual housing and a caravan park in the centre.

The church of St James is built on a slight rise. Dating from the 14th-15th century with a low tower, it has a south transept. All the windows are 19th century.

Reynalton Congregational Chapel is situated on the T-junction. Built in 1867, and rebuilt in 1906 in a simple late Vernacular style with gable entry.

A former mining village, Reynalton was connected to Saundersfoot by a narrow gauge railway until 1939, when with the coal mine closed the line was taken up to be used in the war effort. Reynalton Colliery was a drift mine with the workings in a field behind the houses opposite the church.

Rhodiad-y-brenin

Rhodiad-y-brenin is a small hamlet a mile and a half north-east of St David's Cathedral. The name means 'Royal Road'. There are some appealing older cottages and the Independent Chapel, which was built in 1784 and refurbished in 1884. It closed in 1992 and was converted for residential use, but is Grade II Listed as a rare example of a rural 18th century chapel. Built in the style of a house, rather than a religious building, with an entrance through the long wall of the chapel, rather than the gable end.

To the east of the road is Melin Gwrhyd, a corn mill on the River Alun.

Rhoscrowther

The village of Rhoscrowther, on the eastern side of Angle Bay, all but disappeared under the BP Oil Refinery built in 1961, the church of St

Decuman and a few houses being the only remnants. The settlement is ancient and is said to have been the residence of pre-Norman Welsh princes. The derivation of the name is obscure. The Grade I Listed church, which, without a congregation closed in 2004 and since 2005 has been in the hands of the Friends of Friendless Churches, dates from the 13th century with the addition of a 14th century tower. The south-east chapel is dedicated to the Perrot family who lived at nearby Eastington and the north transept chapel to the White family of Henllan. The chapel at the south-west corner is said to be on the site of St Decuman's cell. St Decuman was, according to tradition, born in the village in the 7th century. He crossed to Dunster in Somerset by coracle where the church is dedicated to him. He was martyred in 706 when his head was cut off with a spade. The font is 12th century and there are a number of funerary monuments. While there were Victorian restorations, the church remained relatively intact. An explosion at the refinery in 1993 lifted the roof of the church, but left the windows and stonework intact.

At the entrance to the church is a former school, built in 1851. It is not owned by the Friends. The holy well of St Decumanus lies in a field some 200 yards south-west of the church. There is a stone surround and it appears to have been roofed. The names Decuman and Decumanus appear interchangeable.

A quarter of a mile north-west of the church is Eastington. Established by Iestyn, a grandson of the Welsh King Hywel Dda, it became known as Iestyn's Farm, and subsequently Eastington. A descendant, Elen, married Sir Stephen Perrot and it was occupied by the family for many years. The house was in ruins by the time Fenton visited early in the 19th century. There are the remains of a stone tower, incorporated into a later farmhouse. The gardens were surrounded by a ha-ha. The house and site is today dominated by the storage tanks of the refinery which lie just 150 yards away.

Robeston Wathen

Robeston Wathen, built on a hill, one and a half miles west of Narberth, is today by-passed by the A40. While the village is quieter than it used to be, it has suffered from the drop in trade. There are some businesses, but little housing development. Robeston House behind the church dates from 1780.

St Andrew's Church dates from the 13th-14th century but the slender tapered west tower is the only original part after a rebuilding in the 1840s and a further refurbishment in 1864.

Bush Inn is situated 600 yards west of the village.

The name Robeston Wathen would indicate 'Robes Farm'. While Lewis, in 1833, gives an alternative to 'Wathen' as 'East'; Speed, in 1610, simply records it as Robeston.

Robeston West

Two and a half miles north-west of Milford Haven is Robeston West. Robeston Hall was the 18th century home of the Scourfield family who had previously occupied a property at Moat from the time of Edward I. The Hall burnt down in 1921, though parts of the garden and the recently modernised 18th century barn remain.

The church of St Andrew, on a raised site, has a north aisle and a massive transeptal north tower, though unusually the north aisle extends beyond the east wall of the chancel. The church dates from the 14th century with a rebuilding in the 1860s.

To the south lies the Murco Oil Refinery.

Roch

Roch is situated off the A487 in the west of the county just under two miles south-east of Newgale. The village has grown up around the castle which dates from the second half of the 13th century. It was built by Adam de Rupe on an outcrop of volcanic rock, according to legend, because of a prophecy that he would die from an adder's bite. The prophecy came true when an adder was carried in to the castle in a basket of wood. The de Rupes were in French the family de la Roche and had extensive lands in Pembrokeshire from 1200. They traced their family back to Charlemagne, the Holy Roman Emperor of the 9th century and the Counts of Flanders.

The castle marks the Landsker line and while built for defence, with its D shaped structure, had later been converted to a comfortable residence. At the time of the English Civil War the castle was owned by the Walter family. Garrisoned by the Royalists, it changed hands three times and suffered damage which was not repaired. The Walters had moved to Rotterdam where Lucy Walters had a son, James, by Prince Charles, the later Charles II. James was created Duke of Monmouth and was the leader of the ill fated Monmouth Rebellion in 1685. By the time of Fenton's visit in 1810 it was in ruins, but from 1900 John Philipps, 1st Viscount St David, and subsequent owners have undertaken substantial renovations. Today it is operated by the Retreats Group as holiday accommodation and a venue for weddings and corporate events.

The church of St Mary dates from the 19th century, though on the site of a much older church.

Apart from the buildings near the castle, the village is almost entirely composed of modern properties. In a field to the east of Grass Holm View is the Lady Well, though there is no stonework or history attached to the well.

Rosebush

Rosebush is a small former slate quarrying village, a mile north of Maenclochog. Today it is best known as the location of Tafarn Sinc, the highest pub in Pembrokeshire, clad in red painted zinc. Dating from 1876, it was built as the Precelly Hotel, serving the small railway station. To attract visitors it had a pleasure garden and lake which now forms part of the Rosebush Caravan Park. It was closed in 1992 but reopened as the Tafarn Sinc and is now a listed building and tourist attraction in its own right.

The railway formed a loop, passing between the Tafarn Sinc and Rosebush Lake. The station or, more properly, halt has been recreated. Remains of the slate quarries are to the north and there are a number of workers' cottages.

Half a mile away from the village is Rosebush Reservoir. Formed by damming the Afon Syfynwy, the reservoir supplies water to North Pembrokeshire and is stocked with brown trout. Day tickets for fishing are available from Llys y Frân Country Park four miles to the south-west.

Rosemarket

Situated two miles north-west of Neyland, Rosemarket is an example of a Norman planned village. The name is probably a corruption of Roose Market, Roose being the old Hundred or administrative area. Established for Flemish settlers following the Conquest, it had a typical Norman layout, with a main street, church and village green. Middle Street retains much of the character with some delightful cottages, but 20th century planners were not as kind to the village as their Norman predecessors.

The Church of St Ishmael is at the southern entrance to the village and retains much of its 12th century original work. There is a western bellcote, an unusually large squint passage, north transept and the chancel is comparatively low. The church underwent 19th century renovation.

South of the church are the earthworks of an Iron Age defended settlement with double banks to the north.

Rosemarket was the site of a mansion owned by Sir Richard Walter, owner of Roch Castle, whose daughter Lucy was the mother of the Duke of Monmouth. The property was in ruins by the time of Fenton's visit in 1810. The only remnant is the Dovecote which stands in a field 135 yards north-west of the church. Built in the 13th-14th century when the village was in the ownership of the Knights Hospitallers, it formed part of the estate of the Great House after the Reformation. With a conical roof, the Dovecote has some 200 nesting boxes.

The Huntsman Inn in West Street is early 20th century, but the pub sign is a painted cast-iron fireback, dating from 1649, depicting General Fairfax, the head of the Roundhead Army.

Tabernacle Chapel in Middle Street was built prior to 1800 though the present building dates from 1885.

Rudbaxton

Rudbaxton is an ancient parish with the church of St Michael just off the A40, three and a half miles north of Haverfordwest. In 1833 there were over 600 inhabitants, but today there are just a few farms. The name was given as 'Rodeparkston' in 1398. The actual derivation is from Alexander Rudepac who granted the land to the Knights of St John at Slebech.

The church is large, with a double aisle and a white washed tower. Originally dedicated to St Madoc and built on a Celtic *llan*, the building dates from the 15th century, with 19th century refurbishments and 20th century fittings. The 17th century monument to the Hayward family, in the south aisle, of three full length figures bearing skulls set into recesses is particularly interesting. It is depicted on a lithograph by John Piper, entitled *Rudbaxton Pembrokeshire, 17th Century Monument 19th Century Furnishing* and is in the collection at the Tate Gallery.

To the east of the church are the remains of a motte, about eight foot high. Rudbaxton Water flows past the village into the Western Cleddau.

There were two mansions in the parish, Withy Bush which disappeared under the airfield of the same name and Poyston, the birthplace of Lieutenant-General Sir Thomas Picton, GCB, who was killed at Waterloo. General Picton was born in 1758. An army officer from the age of 15, Picton went out to the West Indies in 1794 taking part in the capture of

St Vincent. He was appointed Governor of Trinidad where he gained a reputation for brutality and torture (the torture known as pictoning is named after him). He returned to Britain and was tried on 35 counts in 1806, but found guilty on only one and was acquitted on that charge on retrial. Now a Major General, after service in the Netherlands as Governor of Flushing, Picton joined Wellington in Spain and became celebrated as a successful commander in battle distinguishing himself at Busaco, the Battle of Fuentes de Onoro, Ciudad Rodrigo, Badajoz and Vittoria. He was honoured by Parliament, became a KB and GCB (Knight of the Order of the Bath and Knight Grand Cross of the Order of the Bath). In 1815 Picton accepted a high command in the Anglo-Dutch army. He was wounded at Quatre Bras two days before Waterloo, but concealed his injuries and commanded his troops in the battle. Because his luggage had been delayed, he took the field in civilian clothes and a top hat. He was killed when a musket ball hit his temple. A monument was erected to his memory in St Paul's Cathedral, where his remains were transferred in 1859, by order of Parliament and in Carmarthen the Picton memorial was completed in 1828 following a public subscription started in 1823, the King contributing 100 Guineas. Sir Thomas is the only Welshman buried in St Paul's Cathedral.

Sageston

Sageston, now by-passed by the A477, lies half a mile east of Carew Castle. The village has expanded considerably with just a few older houses at the eastern end of the village, including the Plough Inn, an old coaching inn. Sageston Primary School serves a wide area.

South of the A477 is Carew Cheriton Airfield. Developed in 1916 as Milford Airship Station, the airfield was developed in the 1930s to complement the Pembroke Dock Flying Boat Station. From 1939 it was a base for coastal patrols and also as a testing station for new weaponry and, from 1942, acted as a base for towing targets for the Manorbier School of Anti Aircraft Defence and for the Radio Direction Finding School. The station was closed in 1945 and is now used for various commercial purposes, including a karting track and caravan sales.

St Bride's

St Bride's is a scattered settlement at the southern end of St Bride's Bay. It once had a thriving herring fishery. There was a small chapel in which the fishermen prayed but this was converted into a salt house after which the fishery declined. Fenton quotes the couplet:

*"When St Bride's Chapel a salt house was made,
St Bride's lost the herring trade."*

Mary Morgan describes her first view of St Bride's Bay in August 1791 "the sea suddenly broke into my sight at St Bride's Bay, and presented the grandest assemblage of objects that can meet together in one view. The bay is like an immense basin, filled with crystal water, and begirt on every side, except where it opens to the main ocean, with rocks, promontories and mountains. The coves and bays that are formed by those projections, give the most charming variety to the scene, and entirely take away that dreariness and horror which the sea on a flat coast naturally inspires. The water in this basin is perfectly unruffled, and the vessels seem to repose securely on the bosom of the deep. Some with their tall masts glide swiftly into port; whilst others, at a distance, peeping behind the lofty rocks, promise a perpetual succession of commerce and society."

St Bride's was the home of John de St Bride, a descendant of a Norman knight. He was a supporter of Henry Tudor and fought at the Battle of Bosworth with his son in law, a member of the Laugharne family. Fenton relates a story that the young Laugharne, a Cornishman, was washed up on the shore at St Bride's and was discovered by the daughter of John de St Bride, they fell in love and married. The Laugharne family had however been in Pembrokeshire for hundreds of years before this alleged incident and had married into a number of the leading families. The family home was St Bride's House, in ruins at the time of Fenton, but garden features remain to the east of the church.

With the death of John Laugharne in 1715, the estate was divided between his three daughters and the St Bride's property passed to the wife of Charles Philipps, who abandoned the house and built Hill Mansion to the west of the church. This was extended in the 19th century when the estate passed to Lord Kensington and St Bride's Castle was built on the site. The castle became a hospital before being taken over by the Holiday Property Bond to become a form of time-share holiday accommodation.

The church of St Bridget dates from the 13th or 14th century. Today its form is of a nave, chancel and north transept with two double bellcotes and can be attributed to a major rebuilding in 1868. Fenton however describes it as having a tower.

The cliffs here were the site of a Stone Age 'flint factory' which Edward Laws reported in 1888 as "an actual stratification of worked flint chips and flakes, and so careful was this workman, that hitherto, I believe, no spoiled implement has been discovered, though many people have examined and worked at the deposit."

St Dogmael's

St Dogmael's is a large village standing on the southern shore of the Teifi estuary in the north of the county. The main road through the village climbs through mainly late Victorian and Edwardian houses before dropping back down to the estuary where there are modern houses and a jetty. The road continues to Poppit Sands, a popular bathing beach. Other streets climb further up the hill to offer views over Ceredigion. The village boasts a number of pubs and small shops.

Dogmael was the grandson of Ceredig, after whom the county is named, and a great grandson of Brychan Brycheiniog. St Dogmael founded a monastery about a mile from the Norman Abbey, high above the estuary, in a field known as *yr hen monachlog* (the old monastery).

The ruins of St Dogmael's Abbey and the parish church lie off Church Street, where there is limited parking. The Abbey, dedicated to St Mary was founded as a Benedictine House, under the Abbey of Tiron in Normandy. It was originally founded as a Priory in 1113 by Robert Fitzmartin of Tours, Lord of Cemaes, which became St Mary's Abbey in 1120. Fitzmartin's son, endowed the abbey with lands.

Initially, the monks at St Dogmael's came from France with over twenty at the time of its founding. Local wars caused damage and hardship that was exacerbated by a visitation of the Black Death in 1349. By the turn of the 15th century there were just four monks at St Dogmael's and in 1402 Guy, Bishop of St David's accused the Abbot of keeping a monastery of "drunk, gluttonous and lecherous monks". While things improved slightly, at the time of the Dissolution in 1536 there were just eight monks and the abbot at the Abbey.

The abbey site is on an unusually steep slope which may explain its lack of a west door. It is jointly in the care of Cadw and the Church in Wales. The Abbey was dissolved in 1536 and ownership transferred to John Bradshaw of Presteigne who built a mansion from the abbey stone, though by 1603 this had fallen into ruin and today no evidence of its existence remains. There are extensive ruins of the cruciform layout of the Abbey and other buildings, thought to have been a refectory and an infirmary. There is a visitors'centre in the old coach house.

The present Church is dedicated to St Thomas the Apostle, built 1848-52 to a design by Arthur Ashpitel.

Inside the church is the Sagranus Stone, with inscriptions in Latin and Ogham and which provided the key to deciphering the Ogham language. The stone reads 'Sagrani Filus Cunotami' and in Ogham 'Sagramni maqi Cunatami' and there has been conjecture that Sagrani is interchangeable with Dogmael both implying an artificer. The stone has been used as a gatepost and a bridge over a stream. The legend was that as a bridge, a white lady was seen constantly crossing it at midnight. It was discovered in a wall adjoining his house by a former vicar of St Dogmael's, the Revd H. J. Vincent.

Off Poppit Sands are the remains of a V-shaped wooden fish trap which would have supplied the monks with their fish. It is most clearly visible at low tide. Nearby is Cei Bach a small harbour sheltering the boat house. Penrhyn Castle was a coastguard station but is now a private house

In Mill Street is a corn mill dating from the 1640s. The wheel dates from 1860 and since a restoration in 1980, the mill has been operated commercially and is open to the public.

The 18th and 19th centuries saw St Dogmael's develop as a small port, and shipbuilding centre.

The Welsh name for St Dogmael's is Llandudoch, possibly referring to St Tydecho. Llandudoch was the site of an important battle in 1091, when Rhys ap Tewdor, King of Deheubarth (the kingdom covering South West Wales), defeated rebels under Gruffydd ap Maredudd ab Owain.

Plas Newydd, south-east of the village, is a mansion built for Sir Watkin Lewes. Sir Watkin was the second son of a Pembrokeshire clergyman and, after graduating at Cambridge in 1759, was called to the Bar in 1766. He was Member of Parliament for London 1781-96 and Lord Mayor in 1780. He built Plas Newydd as a country retreat. He had however spent a great deal of money getting himself elected and ended up after 1804 in the Fleet prison for debt.

At Trenewydd, south of St Dogmael's there was a tragic accident in 1815 when a quarryman "was incautiously filling a flask with gunpowder from a barrel containing nearly 40lbs of the same and his infant child being about 12 months old, being at the mother's knee, playing with a small stick, one end of which was on fire, a spark was communicated to the powder, which instantly exploded, carrying away the roof of the cottage and blowing up the poor woman, who fell across one of the beams. She was dreadfully scorched and her nose completely crushed; the man was forced through a partition wall, being shockingly burnt and bruised, and the poor babe, who was the unhappy but innocent cause of this complicated calamity, exhibited such a lamentable spectacle of disfigurement, as to agonize the feelings of all who witnessed the afflicting scene. To the further sufferings of father and child, death has put a period, but the poor woman, notwithstanding the injury she sustained was alive on Wednesday week." *The Examiner.*

The parish of St Dogmael's was reputed to be the home of fairies, who would lead men astray at night. It was a common experience for men to have "marvellous adventures and un-tellable trampings, which seemed as thought they would be endless, to find that when day broke, they were close to their own homes". Sikes records that "a severe and dignified clerical person, no longer in the frisky time of life, but advanced in years, was forced one night to join in the magic dance of St Dogmell's and keep it up until daybreak". This echoes a number of stories of fairy rings in Wales where if one set foot in the circle, you were forced to dance with the fairies. In some cases men were alleged to have disappeared for years, in one case in Carmarthenshire it was said that when the spell was broken, the man collapsed and died and his body turned to dust.

St Edrins

St Edrins was a parish in central Pembrokeshire, ten miles north-west of Haverfordwest. The parish church is located three quarters of a mile north-west of Newton in a field next to the road to Treddiog. Declared redundant in 1987 and now a private dwelling, the church was rebuilt in 1846 with a tower, nave and chancel. It stands in the centre of a classic Celtic *llan*. Inside is a 6th-7th century inscribed stone known as St Edrin's Stone or the Alpha and Omega Stone. It is inscribed with a cross and the Greek alpha and omega letters a symbolism often used in early Christianity. St Edrin was the son of a Welsh prince who became a monk in the 7th century.

In the churchyard are the remains of a Holy Well, the waters of which were alleged to cure madness. Eating the grass in the churchyard was supposedly a preventative for men and cattle from the effects of the bite from a mad dog. Cows were turned in to the churchyard to graze while people ate the grass in a sandwich. In the church is a hole in the chancel wall where people left money for the parish clerk in return for eating the grass.

St Elvis

St Elvis was the smallest parish in Wales, consisting of just two farms amounting to less than 200 acres. Situated less than three quarters of a mile east of Solva, St Elvis Farm is the site of the ruined church. Fenton attributes its dedication to St Elwys, though others record it as to St Teilaw or St Teilo.

According to legend, St Elvis, Welsh 'Eilffyw', is identified as St Ailbhe of Munster who baptized St David in the well which is now situated in the farmyard of St Elvis Farm. Tradition was that the well had healing properties and the curative properties were enhanced by sleeping on the nearby capstone. If, however, the patient was visited by a bird called Caladruis, then the cure would not succeed.

The church was dedicated to St Teilo, the site was marked by a few bramble-grown foundations in the yard of St. Elvis farm in 1921. The last wedding was in 1822. The church was 35 feet by 17 feet with a south porch. Burials were to the north of the church.

There is a Neolithic chambered tomb, not in good condition as it was blown up and stones removed by a tenant in 1890, but there are two capstones, one measuring 12 foot by 10 foot. In the late 16th to early 17th century John Voyle and his son in law, Sir Thomas Canon, attempted, unsuccessfully, to mine silver on the Dinas Fawr headland and there are signs of their activities in the form of adits.

To the east of St Elvis Farm is Lochvane. Fenton states that there was a cromlech on the farm at Llechvane. There is no evidence of this, but it is listed as a 'findspot' for Neolithic items.

This is the only known St Elvis in the British Isles and coupled with the Preseli Mountains the combination has given rise to speculation that Elvis Presley's ancestors came from the area.

St Florence

St Florence is a medieval village with traces of its Flemish origins scattered throughout. Situated three miles west of Tenby, it is hard to imagine that this tranquil inland village was once a thriving port, but until John Owen of Orielton built the Penally Embankment in 1811, the River Ritec formed a tidal inlet as far as St Florence.

Field names suggest that there was once a castle locally, but no physical evidence remains.

There are a number of cottages with the round, so-called Flemish chimneys, including the Old Chimneys house near the Sun Inn, and another in Cross Street.

The village was the site of a minor battle in the English Civil War when Royalist forces under Lord Carbery met Parliamentary troops under Colonel Laugharne. Evidence was found in 1964 in the form of cannon balls near the Sun Inn, while a three inch ball was found in the gable wall of Shirley Cottage in the 1990s.

St Florence Church is 12th century in origin, but was enlarged in the 13th century with the four storey tower added in the 15th century. It was extensively restored in the 1870s after the Revd Birket arrived to find a horse stabled in the porch and chickens roosting in the church. There is a squint and the south transept, designed as a mortuary chapel, is divided from the chancel by two low arches with the tower above.

There are two pubs in the village and Elm Court Country House Hotel. To the north of the village is the St Florence Cheese Centre at Ivy Tower Farm. Timmins stayed in the village and relates the following : "mine hostess tells of quaint old customs that, until only the other day, survived in this quiet countryside. I mind the time," says she, "when I was a girl, when there used to be a Vanity Fair in the village every Michaelmas tide. It lasted three whole days, and the men and maids would turn out in their best then, and all the house must be smartened up and put in order; and Squire, he give every working man in the place a bran-new suit of clothes to his back. Ah, there was fine doings then, and I've a-hard tell that they'd used to run a keg of spirits, or what not, from the big cellars down Tenby way. But that was afore my time."

To the north of the village is Manor House Wildlife Park, run by TV star Anna Ryder Richardson and her husband and featured on a number of television series.

On the eastern outskirts of the village are the remains of the Old Mill. The mill was in use in 1609 and continued until the 1840s when William Athoe was the miller. It was converted into a dwelling when grain prices fell, but is now just a shell.

St Ishmael's

St Ishmael's is an ancient village above the cliffs of Milford Haven between Dale and Herbrandston. Expansion in the latter half of the 20th century has not always been in keeping of this ancient village, with an estate called 'Brookside' hardly in keeping with a village with the main street named Burgage Green Road.

The church of St Ishmael lies nearly half a mile south-west of the village in a wooded valley which leads to Monk Haven. A church was established here in the 6th century and was mentioned in the 10th century Laws of Hywel Dda, as being one of the seven bishops' houses of Dyfed. The church dates from the early 12th century and has a nave, chancel and north and south transepts of unequal size, each with a squint. The bellcote has two bells. The church was restored in the 19th century. It is noted for its setting with a stream running through the churchyard. Ishmael or Ismael was believed to have been a disciple of St Teilo and consecrated a bishop by him.

Monk Haven Manor next to the church was built in 1835 as the vicarage.

To the north of the village is St Ishmael's Tump, the remains of a Norman motte and bailey castle. 100 foot in diameter and 16 foot high, it is now covered by trees.

A mile north of the village is Great Hoaten Farm where a huge 17 foot anchor, claimed to be from the Spanish Armada, was laid on the lawn and painted at regular intervals by the Pembrokeshire Association for the Preservation of Ancient Monuments.

At Watch House Point to the south of the village there were a number of WW II minefields and military installations.

In a field next to St Ishmael's Nursery and Garden Centre is the ten foot high red sandstone Bronze Age standing stone, known as the Longstone.

The Brook Inn, with its garden alongside the brook, is situated in Trewarren Road at the eastern side of the village. Trewarren Road leads west to Trewarren House, the home of the Warren Davis family.

St Issells

St Issells or Llanusyllt is an old parish with its church half a mile north of Saundersfoot on the B4316. The parish extended to the sands of Saundersfoot and was a major source of iron ore, clay and anthracite in the 18th and 19th centuries.

The church stands in a valley and dates back to the 13th century with the chancel, north aisle and arcades added a century later. The tower is of stone, but the nave and chancel contain local bricks.

In the churchyard is a preaching cross. The shaft is a replacement but the head and steps are largely original.

In the 1861 *Book of South Wales, the Wye and the Coast*, Mrs S. C. Hall describes the scene: "The church is small but has a tall square tower of grey stone; a tiny stream brawls across the pebbly road, and passes with a whispering rush through the tunnel arch of a rustic footbridge. It is in a pleasant dell environed by trees; in the crowded churchyard lie the hamlet's 'rude forefathers'. The rivulet on the day of our visit, scarcely covered the stepping stones, but at times it becomes a fierce and rapid current, and then the quaint footbridge is the protector of wayfarers. A carter was watering his horses there as we lingered to admire the masses of wild flowers on its banks." The stream still flows through the graveyard, but the stepping stones and footbridge have disappeared. A year after Mrs Hall's visit, F.R. Kempson was commissioned to renovate the church which is not now so small.

To the east of the church is the Hean Castle estate and the Victorian mansion of Hean Castle. Built on the site of the Iron Age fort of Hencastell (Old Castle) which gives Hean Castle its name, it was purchased in 1863 by Charles Vickerman, the son of the treasurer of the Saundersfoot Railway. Vickerman extended the 1840 house in the style of a Tudor fortified house using red sandstone and Forest of Dean stone. It has turrets and a tower. It was sold in 1899 to Sir William Thomas Lewis, 1st Baron Merthyr who had made his money from the coal industry in the Rhondda Valley, where the he owned the Lewis Merthyr Consolidated Collieries, and remains in his family.

In 1781, George Williams of this parish, a married man and collier by trade was tried for the murder of Sarah Powell. She was pregnant by him and he provided her with a potion intended to procure an abortion which operated so strongly that it killed her. His defence lawyer argued that she had taken the potion willingly and it was therefore 'self murder'. Williams was acquitted, but the court was not told that following an exhumation and post mortem carried out on a table in the church, witnessed by her family, it was found that the potion contained powdered glass and iron rust mixed with treacle. It was recorded that the girl had taken several days to die.

St Nicholas (Tremarchog)

St Nicholas is a small attractive village three and a half miles south-west of Fishguard. The church at the centre of the village has a nave, chancel and south transept with a buttressed west bellcote. Inside are three early Christian stones. One, which was used as a stile, has the Latin inscription 'Tunccetace uxsor daari hic iacet' – 'Here lies Tunccetace, wife of Daarus' and is known as the Tunccetace stone. The other two were used as gateposts on a local farm and have inscribed crosses, one with the name 'Paani'.

The village has some attractive cottages and little modern development.

Half a mile south-east of the village is Ffyst Samson, a Neolithic chambered burial chamber with a capstone of white spar stone measuring seven foot by four foot supported on just two six foot orthostats. Fenton recorded the cromlech as being on high ground near the village of Trellys, which is now just a farm.

To the east of the village is Rhos y Clegyrn, where the is a nine foot standing stone and evidence of a second stone marking a possible Bronze Age cremation site. To the south-west is evidence of a circular enclosure and to the north-east is a ring barrow.

St Petrox

St Petrox is a church lying 2.3 miles south of Pembroke with the Rectory being the only other building nearby. The dedication is to St Petrox or Petrocus, a saint from South Wales who is more usually associated with Devon and Cornwall. Parts of the church including the tower date from the 13th century. It was extensively refurbished in 1854 by the architect R.K. Penson, at the expense of Earl Cawdor. The church tower tapers and there is a central bellcote.

St Twynnells

St Twynnells is a small village a little over a mile west of St Petrox. Originally consisting of just a few farms and cottages there has been significant development in recent years. The church, granted to the Bishop of St David's in 1260, has been variously dedicated to St Deiniol and St Gwynog or St Wynnoc, the latter being the derivation of the village name. The three storey church tower commands extensive views. The church was refurbished by Earl Cawdor in 1858 with the architect David Brandon. The church has a long barrel vaulted nave and chancel with squint to the south transept.

To the west of the village are the deserted remnants of RAF St Twynnells, a radar station built in 1940, with a series of blockhouses, though much of the structure was below ground level.

Sardis

There are two hamlets named Sardis in Pembrokeshire. Between Rosemarket and Hill Mountain, Sardis is a hamlet around a cross roads. There are a number of older houses with small developments of modern housing.

The other Sardis lies, south of Stepaside, on a country road near Hean Castle. There is an unusual Congregational church built in 1825 with a small round tower. Housing is relatively modern.

Saundersfoot

Saundersfoot was originally part of the parish of St Issel and known as Coedrath. There were just a few cottages as the area was part of the hunting forest for the Earls of Pembroke. Records show that in 1332 Walter Elisaunder paid rent for the water and the name Saundersfoot is derived from his name. Coal was mined in the vicinity as far back as 1324 and this industry expanded rapidly in the 18th century. In 1829 the Saundersfoot Railway and Harbour Company was established by statute. Two tram roads were built for coal trams, one using horse drawn trams, the other using gravity, with full trams going down hill hauling up the empty trams. The principal shareholder of the Railway and Harbour Company was Sir Richard Bulkeley Philipps of Picton Castle. The Strand was originally known as Railway Street, with the railway running along the middle of the street. In the 1870s the tramway was converted to a steam railway. Saundersfoot Harbour was operational by 1830 with five jetties. The coal industry started to decline in the mid 1850s though mining continued until 1939. The village gradually transformed from an industrial port to a seaside resort, helped by the coming of the Great Western Railway and Saundersfoot is today the most popular resort in the county after Tenby.

Saundersfoot has the appearance of a small seaside town rather than a village with new housing to the west and apartment buildings at the eastern end of the Strand. The harbour is now used by pleasure craft and there are some interesting older buildings. The sandy beach is Saundersfoot's main attraction and the visitors have an array of pubs, bars restaurants and hotels as well as local shops and amusement arcades. There are a number of caravan and chalet parks away from the seafront.

At the end of the Strand is the old rail tunnel that led to Wiseman's Bridge, now part of a public footpath. The track of the gravity tramroad is known as the Incline and is now a footpath leading from Brookland Place.

Scleddau

Scleddau is situated two miles south of Fishguard on the A40. The present village sprang up along the Turnpike Road which was built in 1797. The pub, the Gate Inn, refers to the old turnpike gate which stood here. There has been modern development off the main road. Sion Chapel, built in 1859 in Chapel Road, appears neglected.

The village takes its name from the Western Cleddau river which rises nearby.

The original village, known as Llanstinan was centred around the now abandoned little church of St Justinian a little over half a mile east of the present village. Built on the traditional Celtic *llan*, the church today is only accessible by a footpath. The church consists of a nave, chancel and south transept with a squint. The building dates from the 13th century though the windows are 18th century. George Owen's map of 1603 shows the village surrounding the church and outlines of cottages and houses can still be seen in the vicinity.

500 yards south of the church is Parc y Castell, a field which contains an Iron Age defended enclosure some 70 yards in diameter.

There were three mansions in the area, Ciliauwen, Langton Hall and Pant y Phillip.

Simpson Cross

Simpson Cross is a largely modern village on the Haverfordwest to St David's road, two miles south-east of Roch. Most of the development lies to the north of the main road. There is an art gallery and the Pembrokeshire Motor Museum. There is no pub or place of worship.

Slebech

Passing along the A40, five miles west of Narberth, Slebech is today evidenced by the large disused church and a small retail park. The parish however has played an important role in the history of Pembrokeshire for over 800 years. Situated on the north-western bank of the Eastern Cleddau, Slebech was granted to the Knights Hospitallers of the Order of St John of Jerusalem, who built the church of St John the Baptist on the banks of the Cleddau, one mile south of the A40, in 1161. The Knights were granted the rights to a number of other parishes and their commandery was established at Slebech which was used by pilgrims and mendicants until the dissolution of the monasteries under Henry VIII in 1536. The St John Ambulance charity evolved from the Order of St John, though today it has no religious affiliation.

The Slebech estate was bought from the crown by Roger Barlow in 1546. Roger was one of the four children of John Barlow, imprisoned in the Tower of London, charged with high treason by Henry VII. Roger, having been left destitute, went to Spain from where, in the employ of the Emperor Charles V, he sailed to South America and discovered Peru. He was ordered home by Henry VIII and later appointed Vice Admiral to Lord Seymour. Meanwhile his bother William had been appointed Bishop of St David's in 1536 before translating to Bath and Wells in 1548. The Barlow family built Slebech Mansion near the site of the Knights' Commandery and continued to live there until the 18th century when it passed through several hands before coming into the ownership of Nathaniel Phillips. Phillips, the illegitimate son of a merchant, went to Jamaica in 1759 at the age of 26 and over 25 years accumulated a fortune through the sugar plantations and slavery. He purchased Slebech from William Knox, a bankrupt slaver, in 1793 together with a further 600 acres. Slebech Hall was rebuilt and in 1796 Phillips married Mary Philipps, 40 years his junior by whom he had two sons and two daughters. The family continued to operate the Jamaican estates until the end of slavery in 1834. The estate passed to Mary Dorothea and her sister Louisa, the Countess of Lichfield. Mary Dorothea married Baron de Rutzen in 1822 and they became Lords of the Manor of Slebech.

The 1161 church of St John the Baptist, in the grounds of the house became the subject of a court case between the Bishop of St David's and Baron de Rutzen. The Baron had removed the roof of the church without authority and was instructed to reinstate it. It is not recorded whether any reinstatement took place, but the church today with its Norman tower is roofless, though a service is held there on an annual basis. It is still owned by the Knights of St John and a footpath leads to the church from Blackpool Mill. Baron de Rutzen funded the much larger church of St John the Baptist on the A40. Accommodating 500 worshippers, the church was designed by J.H. Good. It was closed in 1990 due to subsidence.

There have been marriages between the owners of Slebech and the Philipps of Picton Castle on a number of occasions over the years and the two estates were linked again by marriage in the 1930s and after being sold out of the family for a time was bought back and converted into a hotel by Geoffrey and Georgina Philipps.

One and a half miles away from Slebech Hall is Picton Castle, founded by Sir William de Picton in the reign of William II. The original wooden castle was built on high ground at the confluence of the East and Western Cleddau rivers.

The Picton Castle which stands today was built in the late 13th century by Sir John Wogan, Justicar of Ireland. The design was unusual in that it had no courtyard, but seven projecting round towers. An earlier castle was built by Wizo about half a mile west of the present building. Picton was attacked by French troops during the Glyndwr Rebellion and changed hands during the English Civil War. The castle has altered little over the years. It became the centre of power in Pembrokeshire with its owners acting as Lord Lieutenant and Members of Parliament. With the changing years, the living quarters became more comfortable and a new entrance was constructed, but much of the original building remains. By marriages of heiresses first to Owain Dwnn and subsequently to Sir Thomas Philipps of Cilsant in the late 15th century the castle passed to the Philipps family and is still owned by that family, though a number of inheritors, through marriage, have adopted the Philipps name. The castle and its gardens are open daily during the summer months with guided tours of the castle each afternoon.

Solva

Solva, situated on the north of St Bride's Bay, is one of the most attractive villages in the county. It is believed that the Vikings used Solva as a harbour and its name is derived from the Norse for 'sunny inlet'. Solva is popular for holiday homes with 21% of properties being second homes.

Divided into Lower and Upper Solva, it has an outstanding setting, in a deep ravine with rocks sheltering the harbour from storms. Fenton describes how the harbour "by a singular bend it takes at the mouth, when once entered, is well protected from the violence of the sea, and furnishes excellent shelter for shipping, but the entrance is dangerous, having a large pyramidical rock that divides the passage, leaving a narrow opening on each side". He describes Upper Solva as commanding "a most delightful view of that almost land-locked expanse of ocean, Bride's Bay, and begins to be frequented in the summer months by such as wish for an airy, healthy situation, with a charming sea prospect."

Fenton is less complimentary of Lower Solva, which was then an active port, taking ships of up to 250 tons. Until the coming of the railways, the port thrived with nine warehouses and 12 limekilns. In 1848 between 300 and 500 emigrants boarded the little ship, *Cradle*, to sail from Solva to New York. The fare was £3, but passengers had to provide their own food, a problem as the voyage could take between four and sixteen weeks.

The coast nearby was dangerous, not just because of the rocks. On 8th January, 1773, the *Phoebe and Peggy*, a fully rigged ship en route from Philadelphia to Liverpool was wrecked off Porth y Bwlch, Solva and all survivors murdered for their valuables.

Today the picturesque harbour of Solva bustles with pleasure craft and the village is popular with walkers. The approach to Lower Solva from Middle Mill passes through Prendergast, with its pretty cottages overlooking the Solva River, before the collection of old inns and galleries that make up Main Street, leading to the harbour and its car park. Apart from the bridge on the main A 487 road leading into Solva from Newgale, just ahead of which are the remains of a corn mill, there are two further bridges across the river leading to the Gribin, where at the point is an Iron Age promontory fort. Also on this side of the harbour is a set of four linked lime kilns. Main Street rises above the harbour to Upper Solva with its chapels, inns and terraced cottages before leading to the more modern developments around the village.

St Aidan's Church was built in 1888 and is notable for the architect, John Loughborough Pearson, the prominent Victorian church architect, whose work includes Bristol, Chichester, Lincoln, Truro, Peterborough and Exeter Cathedrals, St George's Chapel, Windsor, Westminster Hall and Westminster Abbey. Pearson used colourful materials, including green granite from Middle Mill and yellow Doulting stone. The east window is by the noted London manufacturer Clayton and Bell, while the font is from the 12th century church of St Elvis, as is the cross in the porch. The church is a simple layout with a single width nave and chancel, the chancel marked from the exterior with windows being stepped up, and a western bellcote.

Pearson was commissioned by Canon Gilbert Harries whose family seat was at Llanunwas, less than half a mile away to the west. Fenton stayed there with Joseph Harries Esq. and describes the estate as stretching from Nine Wells to the estuary of Solva between the A487 and the sea. Today Llanunwas House has been split into flats.

On the coast south-west of Llanunwas is Porth y Rhaw Iron Age promontory fort. While coastal erosion has taken its toll on the site, it was a large enclosure with three banks, with springs on the inland edge providing fresh water. There is evidence of iron working and glass bead manufacture on the site and of at least eight round houses. Finds of Roman material point to the fort continuing to be occupied well into the Roman period. The Pembrokeshire Coastal Footpath passes the site and there is access from Llanunwas and Nine Wells.

Spittal

Spittal is a village to the east of the A40 between Haverfordwest and Fishguard. The name is derived from 'hospital' as it was the site of a *hospitium* for pilgrims established by Bishop Beck in the late 13th century. All trace of the *hospitium* which was situated 100 yards south of the church has been lost.

At the centre of this appealing village is the village green with the nearby pub, The Pump on the Green. Opposite is the old village school, now replaced by a modern area school on the outskirts of the village. Older buildings dominate the centre, but modern developments have increased the size of this peaceful village.

The church of St Mary is medieval in origin but restored on a number of occasions in the Victorian era. In the porch is the Cuniovende Stone. Dating from the 5th or 6th century, it has inscriptions in Ogham and Latin but only the Latin text is visible, reading 'EVALI FILI DENCU/CUNIOVENDE/MATER EIUS' meaning 'Evali son of Dencu set up by his mother Cuniovende'. According to an article in *Archaeologia Cambrensis* the porch was constructed in the 19th century to accommodate the stone. The church has some interesting stained glass windows, including one in memory of Major Archibald Bellairs Higgon of nearby Scolton Manor who was killed at Gallipoli in World War I. The church has an unusually long chancel and there are two bellcotes, one single above the chancel arch, known as the priest's bell and one double above the west wall. There is an interesting recess in the south chancel wall which might have been an Easter Sepulchre or have contained a tomb. There are squints on either side of the chancel arch.

300 yards east of the church is Spittal Rath, an Iron Age defended enclosure, the northern bank of which has surprisingly been built upon with the centre of the rath now a private garden. The mound's local name of Dane Hill may give some clue as to the pre-Norman activities here.

In September 1572 three teenagers discovered a brass crock at Spittal containing ancient treasures of gold and silver. The find was reported by John Wogan, High Sheriff of Pembrokeshire to Lord Burghley: "Jevan Canton ... Hurte and Thomas Probert of this county of Pembroke have ffounde at an old pyre of (walls) at Spittal in the said countie a great quantitie of threasure, gold and silver, conteynede in a certain crockle of brasse as is supposed, and that they had knowledge thereof by advertisement of one Syr Lewis, a prieste dwelling in Carmarthenshire not far from Kayo". It is thought that the find was made in the vicinity of the *hospitium* and that it was a monastic treasure horde.

A little over a mile south-east of Spittal lies Scolton Manor Museum and Park. The house was built in 1842 for the Higgon family who lived there until 1987. The outbuildings display collections representing Pembrokeshire rural life. The cross roads, to the north of the Manor, is known as Gallows Cross, and marks the site of manorial executions.

Square and Compass

Named after the inn on the A487 St David's to Fishguard road, the hamlet of Square and Compass is a ribbon development with farms and a garage and some terraced cottages, just north-east of Mesur y Dorth. The road runs along a ridge giving views of the sea. There are two further tiny hamlets, Pen Parc and Llanon, with no church or chapel, off the main road. There is a large caravan park at Torbant Farm.

Stackpole (See also Cheriton and Bosherston)

The village of Stackpole is three miles south of Pembroke, though it was not the original site for the village. The whole village was moved away from the Stackpole estate in 1735. Stackpole House was situated 500 yards to the west of the village on the opposite side of the lake. Stackpole village has increased in size over recent years and has some old cottages and the Stackpole Inn, with plenty of greenery.

The Stackpole Estate is now owned by the National Trust. The main access to the estate is via Bosherston, while there is parking at Stackpole Quay which is the nearest point to Barafundle Bay, considered by many to be the most beautiful of all Pembrokeshire's beaches.

The first known lord of Stackpole was Elidyr, around 1188 when Giraldus Cambrensis mentions him in connection with the tale of his steward, Simon. Simon had assumed the role of steward without being appointed and for forty days performed his duties and seemed to know his master's desires without instruction. He never slept in the house but was always there in the morning. He never went to church and one night a servant saw him in the graveyard in discussion with demons. When questioned he confessed that his mother had been tricked by a demon and he was the result of their liaison. Elidyr is a Welsh name and it is not impossible that his family retained their estate through the Norman Conquest. The family continued to hold the estate until the 14th century, when through marriage it passed to the Vernon family of Staffordshire. In 1576 it passed to Margaret Vernon who had married Thomas Stanley, second son of the Earl of Derby and she employed Roger Lort as her agent. Lort purchased the estate in 1611.

The Lorts were not popular in the area and were accused of profiting from wrecking. They were litigious but appear to have married well. Roger Lort, grandson of the purchaser switched sides in the English Civil War but was subsequently knighted and given a baronetcy by

Tomb of Sir Elidor

Charles II in 1662. In 1698 the estate passed to Elizabeth Lort who had married Sir Anthony Campbell of Cawdor some ten years earlier. Elizabeth was a widow and ran the estate until her son, John Campbell, was old enough to take over. John extended Stackpole Court and his grandson, also John, who inherited the estate was created Baron Cawdor of Castlemartin in 1796. The family estates which included not only land in Pembrokeshire, but in Scotland, were further increased when, in 1804, John Campbell inherited the vast estates of the Vaughan family in Carmarthenshire.

The Cawdors were one of the wealthiest families in Britain. Stackpole Court was one of the grandest houses in the kingdom and in 1902 the third earl entertained King Edward VII there. Taxes were however to take their toll, coupled with the loss of income caused by the seizure of the Castlemartin Ranges by the Ministry of Defence and, in 1963, the Court was demolished and the estates in Wales were sold off. The family have however left a lasting legacy in the form of the Stackpole Estate.

Stackpole Court was built in 1735 on the foundations of an earlier house, the hall of which became the cellar, and enlarged in the 19th century. When it was demolished in 1963, Earl Cawdor had removed the finest of the internal fittings to Park House, an early 18th century house on the estate. Stackpole Court enjoyed a superb view of the lake which had been created by building a dam at Broad Haven. The eight arched bridge across the lake was built to connect the house with a deer park and to Stackpole Quay. 640 yards west of the house was an ice house, now converted into a grotto.

Stackpole Quay was built in the late 18th century and around the quayside are a lime kiln, warehouse and boat house. There is a picnic area and refreshments are available.

Between the lake and Barafundle Bay are two tumuli and a six foot standing stone known as the Devil's Quoit. Archaeological digs have discovered that the stone is Neolithic in origin, but the site was also of religious significance in the Iron Age.

Near a local farm, according to tradition, Timmins reports "a certain ghostly party of headless travellers were wont to arrive, about nightfall, in a spectral coach from Tenby; each pale shade, as 'tissaid, bearing his head stowed snugly away under his arm!"

There is a legend that three standing stones about a mile from each other, the most easterly being in Stackpole Warren, come together at Sais's Ford on a certain day each year and dance before returning to their original locations.

Star

Star is a delightful hamlet stretching down a hill to the wooded valley of the Afon Cneifa, situated in the north-west of the county, three and a quarter miles south-east of Boncath.

Entering Star from Bwlchygroes, the road takes a sharp turn with Soar Baptist Chapel with its external immersion baptistery on the left. The chapel was built in 1879-81. Continuing down the hill are houses and cottages with attractive gardens and at the foot of the hill, where the road crosses the Cneifa, is the 18th century Star Mill, now converted for holiday accommodation.

Half a mile west of the village stood Dolau Llanerch, the castellated mansion of the Lloyd family. Fenton in 1810 reported that not a trace of the mansion remained with "a neat farmhouse having sprung from its ruins".

Just under half a mile north-east of Star is Clydau Church. Built on a Celtic *llan*, the church is dedicated to St Clydai the virgin daughter of Brychan Brycheiniog, king of what is now Breconshire in the 5th century. Brychan, born in Ireland was the son of Marchell, daughter of the king of Garthmadryn (later renamed Brycheiniog) and Anlach the son of the King Coronac of Ireland. Brychan had a large number of children who became saints and are commemorated in 29 churches in Wales, as well as in Cornwall and Brittany. The churchyard is entered through a lych-gate with stile attached. The church was renovated in 1885 which changed its perspective, in that the pitch of the roof was raised so reducing the effectiveness of the 15th century tower. The nave is double aisled with a very short chancel. There is a 12th century font and 13th century stoup but the most interesting items are three inscribed stones. Dating from the 5th to the 7th century, all three have Latin inscriptions and two also have Ogham script. Of particular interest is the centre stone which reads 'SOLINI FILIUS VENDONI', as Solinus was a missionary who travelled to Ireland in 431 AD and returned to Wales the following year. A little under half a mile north-east of the church is Hendre Cymru, thought to be the site of a medieval township.

The river, the Cneifa, which means the shearer, flows from Star through a wooded valley to join the Cych.

Stepaside

Stepaside today is a pleasant hamlet in a wooded valley running from the A477, Carmarthen to Tenby road, to Wiseman's Bridge on the coast. It is alleged that the name stems from a visit by Oliver Cromwell who demanded that the residents 'Step aside'.

The area was heavily industrialised, coal was mined here in the 14th century and there were up to twelve collieries in the 19th century. Kilgetty Colliery was active until the 1930s and Stepaside Ironworks were established in 1848 and worked intermittently until 1877. Grove colliery was sunk to provide fuel for the ironworks. A tramline was built between Stepaside and Saundersfoot Harbour which was later a steam railway. Today there is no industry, but an Industrial Heritage Park has been established with a walk along the old tramway passing the impressive remains of the ironworks through to Wiseman's Bridge and then through a tunnel to Saundersfoot.

Stepaside has lost its only inn, the Stepaside and the school is now a private residence.

Steynton

The village of Steynton, one of the largest parishes in the county by population in the 1830s, is situated just to the north of Milford Haven town, the expansion of which has meant that the village is now virtually a suburb. The parish of Steynton included the area where the town of Milford Haven grew. Fenton states that it was the "vill of Adam de Stainton".

The village is busy with traffic and there has been considerable modern development. The area around the church has some older properties and the church with its tall tower is imposing. During the English Civil War 20 musketeers were stationed in the tower. Much of this large church, with the exception of the 13th century tower, is a Victorian reconstruction. The Royal Commission on Ancient Monuments in Wales contained the following; "In 1851 Sir Stephen Glynne described this church as "of coarse and rude architecture, with the ordinary amount of mutilation and destruction of original windows". A restoration in 1882 made matters worse, the body of the building being "almost swept out of historical existence by a tornado of change. Excepting mutilated remnants of the main walls and the tower, itself in part falsified, there have survived out of the past only three small windows in the side walls of the chancel. Of the north entrance the north door only remains. Every other feature has been wiped out!" The 1882 restoration did discover some interesting relics however, including "A human skull, three horses' skulls, and a pike-head, found under the second chancel step. The present location of the iron pike-head is unknown. In each pillar of the arcade was found a cavity, and in each cavity a human thigh-bone. These were remains, as much probably of Viking warriors as of British saints. The cavities were about four feet from the ground". The church is again undergoing change to bring it into wider use.

An Ogham stone, the Gendilius Stone is now in the church. In the graveyard is a tomb marked M.O.W. for Man of War. It is the grave of a headless Cromwellian soldier discovered in the 19th century in the vicarage. The church was dedicated to St Kewel or Cewyll and now to St Peter.

On the cross roads is the large Horse and Jockey pub.

Almost forgotten now, Steynton's most famous son was Sir William James. He was born at Bolton Mill in 1722, the son of a poor miller. Educated at Steynton, he exhausted the school's library and was set to work at the mill. His parents realising that this life did not suit him, indentured him to a Bristol trader. He escaped on board an Indiaman and learnt navigation and in due course became the ship's mate. At the age of 20 he was introduced to and married the widow of an East India captain. He then distinguished himself first as captain and then as commodore in the navy of the East India Company. In 1756 he defeated a pirate fleet that had plagued the British for 50 years. On his return to Britain he was made a director of the company and was created a baronet in 1778. He returned to Pembrokeshire and was able to provide for his aged parents. He became Member of Parliament for West Loo, a Fellow of the Royal Society, an elder brother of Trinity House and a governor of Greenwich Hospital. Severndroog Castle at Shooters Hill in Greenwich was built in his memory.

Summerhill

Summerhill is a hamlet between Stepaside and Amroth, just north of the coast. Originally a hill used for the summer grazing of flocks it has expanded considerably from the two early 20th century houses and Cwmrath Farm. There are estates of bungalows on both sides of the road and a caravan park. Summer Hill Primitive Methodist Chapel built in 1897 is now a private home. The village supports a farm shop and stores at Cwmrath Farm and a hairdressing salon.

Sutton

Sutton is a pretty rural hamlet two miles west of Haverfordwest. There are some attractive old cottages and farm buildings and two small modern developments. To the north of Sutton is Bethel Baptist Chapel.

Talbenny

Talbenny is a scattered community on the cliff top at the southern promontory of St Bride's Bay. The name is said to mean 'place at the end'. The church of St Mary the Virgin stands on its own, 270 yards from the sea and 250 feet above sea level. The walls of the nave are 13th century with a 15th century double bellcote. The chancel is from an 1893 renovation, while many of the windows were renewed in the 1970s. There is a Roll of Honour which remembers 82 servicemen who died, when flying from nearby RAF Talbenny, in World War II.

The airfield was established in 1941 and was originally a Coastal Command station linked with Dale. In 1942 the Czech 311 Bomber Squadron arrived and flew Wellingtons, patrolling for U-boats and flying bombing missions against targets in Western France and the Bay of Biscay. After the war the hangars were demolished and the airfield returned to agriculture, but parts of the runways remain.

Tavernspite

Six roads meet at Tavernspite which lies on the eastern border of the county, just under three miles south-west of Whitland. The village takes its name from the inn which Fenton describes as being where post-chaises were kept and the Milford mail stopped to change horses. He went on to describe the situation as "bleak, on the edge of a large tract of uncultivated ground". The origin of the name is uncertain, but Fenton attributes it to Tafarn y Spytty or the inn raised from the ruins of an *hospitium*, said to have been founded by the monks of Whitland who possessed the land. Others dispute this derivation suggesting that the tavern was built to spite a neighbouring tavern. All trace of the original coaching inn has disappeared though there is a modern pub known as the Alpha Inn.

Mary Morgan stayed at the Tavernspite Inn in October 1791, finding it "very dirty and uncomfortable".

The village enjoys views over the vale of Lampeter Velfrey and is now home to two caravan sites and a modern school as well as developments of bungalows.

Tavernspite has one dubious claim to fame. On 6th April, 1801 David Duffield, a 17 year old youth, was hanged, at the Bowling Green in Haverfordwest, for the murder of Ann Morgan, an 11 year old girl. His body was then hung in chains at Tavernspite, the last juvenile in Britain to suffer such a punishment. His execution and gibbeting cost Pembrokeshire £20 7s 4d. The gibbet was erected on a Bronze Age burial mound, Crug Swllt, in a field east of the gardens in Ash Lane.

Templeton

Templeton, on the A 478 two miles south of Narberth, is often ignored by the tourists speeding south to the beaches, but is one of the most interesting villages in the county.

The name is derived from it having been owned by the Knights Templar in the 13th century. Known initially as the Templar's Farm, it was called Villa Temparil in 1282 and a year later as Villa Templarorium Campestris, signifying the presence of some form of religious house belonging to the Templars. There was also reference to burgesses in 1283 while in the 16th century Owen described Templeton as being a borough in decay.

The layout of the old village is one the finest example in Wales of a deliberately planned medieval settlement, with its single main street of houses with plots of land or burgages to the rear with later narrow field strips, which replaced the open field system, still identifiable. There are over twenty listed buildings along the main road, including the 17th century Templeton Farmstead.

St John's Church was built in 1859 on the site of a previous church, possibly the wayside chapel of which Timmins could find no trace in 1895 . It is a typical Victorian edifice of nave, chancel and bellcote. In the churchyard is the upright of an ancient cross.

There is a Baptist Chapel first established in 1667 at Molleston, a mile from the village and the United Reform Church dating from 1819, rebuilt in 1838.

The village retains the Boars Head Inn and there has been considerable modern development away from the main road.

Behind Templeton Farm are the earthworks of Sentence Castle, a small medieval motte and bailey castle. To the north of the castle is Margaret's Well, listed as one of the Holy Wells of Wales, contained in a stone chamber.

South-west of the village is the disused Templeton Airfield, established in 1942 as a satellite to Haverfordwest. Over the next three years it was used by various squadrons including heavy bombers. It closed in August 1945.

Within the boundary of the airfield is said to be the site of the 1081 Battle of Mynydd Carn, when Gruffydd ap Cynan, Prince of Gwynedd and Rhys ap Tewdwr, Prince of Deheubarth, fought against the usurper Trahaiarn of Gwynedd. Gruffydd and Rhys were victorious.

In the late 19th and early 20th century Templeton had a brickworks, founded by William Weston Young, better known as an illustrator of Swansea Porcelain, who had invented a specialised firebrick. The works closed in the 1920s.

Thorne

Thorne is a small hamlet south of the B4319 adjoining the Castlemartin Range and has some attractive cottages. The Calvinistic Methodist Chapel erected in 1812 has now been converted to holiday accommodation. The road is a No Through Road.

Thornton

Thornton is a hamlet, pleasantly situated on the road running from Milford Haven to Robeston West. There is a mix of housing and the English Baptist Chapel is the most notable building. Built in the fork of two roads, the builders took advantage of the natural slope to build a British National School accessible from the Tiers Cross road with the chapel above it appearing as a single storey from the Robeston road. The Chapel was built in 1867.

In the field across the Robeston road from the chapel are the earthworks of Thornton Rath, a semi circular Iron Age defended enclosure.

Tiers Cross

Tiers Cross is a hamlet four miles south-west of Haverfordwest. Built on the cross roads, there is a mix of housing, a pub, the Welcome Traveller and Tabernacle United Reform Church and Congregational Chapel. The chapel was established prior to 1800, rebuilt in 1815 and 1828 and refurbished in 1932, but has the appearance of being well cared for. There is a certain amount of commerce in the village with a garage, tyre service centre and Edwards Coaches garage. To the north is the Bolton Hill stone quarry.

Trecwn

Trecwn lies three miles south of Fishguard. The name translates as town or farmstead of dogs. It was the site of an 18th century mansion owned by the Johnes family which was demolished. The village was formerly known as Llanfair Nant y Gof.

In 1938 the Royal Navvy Armaments Depot was established there. It is thought that its location was never discovered by the Germans. It remained as a naval depot until the 1990s, since when attempts have been made to find a use for it. The depot was extensive, stretching for three quarters of a mile along the valley and having its own narrow gauge rail network servicing 58 caverns. Workers were housed along Barham Road and their children educated in the Barham School. The depot was connected to Fishguard and Milford Haven by rail.

Trecwn Manor gardens can be traced in the land opposite the entrance to the depot. John Wesley preached under an oak tree in the manor grounds in 1777 and there is a commemorative plaque to the east of Barham Road. John Johnes of Trecwn, a cousin of George Owen, was murdered at Newport Fair on 16th June, 1578 by Griffith Philipps of Pentypark apparently as part of a family feud.

The church of Trecwn is located 700 yards south of the bridge over the Nant y Bugail. Built in a circular Celtic *llan*, the church of St Mary was built in 1855, by the Barham family, then owners of Trecwn, replacing a medieval church. It is a simple design of nave and chancel with a north porch and bellcote. In 1929 it was described as a chapel attached to Letterston.

In the valley is Mamre the Calvinistic Methodist Chapel built in 1843 and subsequently rebuilt and refurbished in 1864 and 1909.

A mile and a half south-west of Trecwn is Castle Bucket, a very well delineated Iron Age enclosure some 74 yards in diameter.

Just under a mile north-east of Trecwn is Llygad y Cleddau, or the Eye of the Cleddau, regarded as the source of the Western Cleddau, although the stream which emerges from underground actually rises at Ffynnon Cleddau a little to the south of the farm.

Trefasser

Trefasser is a small farming community on a No Through Road, near the coast south of Strumble Head, four miles west of Fishguard. It was the 'town of Asser'. Asserius Menevensis was born here and educated at St David's before becoming the tutor and biographer of Alfred the Great. He was renowned for his learning and went to Wessex around 884 and was made bishop of Sherborne. He died in 909.

At Trefasser Cross is Castell Poeth, variously described as a motte and bailey castle, defended enclosure and tumulus. Fenton excavated the site and discovered funerary urns while others have discovered a bronze mirror. It is clear that this is a site that has been re-used over the millennia.

Treffgarne

Treffgarne is situated just off the A40 a little over five miles north of Haverfordwest. The name means 'Town of Rocks' because of the Treffgarne Rocks, outbreaks of ancient Ordovician rhyolite volcanic plugs on either side of the Treffgarne Gorge, giving the appearance of castles guarding the gorge. Mary Morgan on her trip to Milford Haven in 1791 described one as resembling a fine gothic cathedral from a distance.

The village is attractive, with the small Meadow Park estate of bungalows developed to the west of the village.

Little Treffgarne lies across the River Cleddau above the Gorge and is believed to have been the birthplace of Owain Glyndwr, the leader of the Welsh rebellion of 1400-1406. Earlier it was the site of a Cistercian monastery, established by Bishop Bernard of St David's in 1144, which had moved to Whitland by 1151.

Treffgarne Hall stands to the west of the village. It was rebuilt in 1824 by its owner, Dr David Evans. The gardens have been restored and on occasions open for charity under the National Gardens Scheme.

Treffgarne church is dedicated to St Michael. A Victorian rebuild, it contains some interesting stained glass windows and has a nave chancel and bellcote.

Treffgarne Lake is now used for canoeing by the Sealyham Activity Centre (see Wolfscastle). It was formed by quarrying for a hard igneous stone, known as adesite that was used for road building. The quarries closed in the 1960s.

North of the village the A40, railway and the Western Cleddau pass through the Treffgarne Gorge which was created during the last Ice Age. Above the Gorge there are no less than eight Iron Age settlements and defended enclosures.

According to legend a cave in Treffgarne Mountain runs 12 miles through to St David's. A dog entered the cave and some time later a scratching was heard under the floor of a cottage in St David's. When the stone was lifted the dog which disappeared in Treffgarne crept out.

Treffynnon

Treffynnon, the name means 'town of springs', is a small farming hamlet one and a quarter miles north-west of Llandeloy in which parish it belongs. The Calvinistic Methodist chapel lies on the north-western outskirts. It was built in 1867 and rebuilt nine years later.

East of the hamlet is Treffynnon Burial Chamber, a Neolithic chambered tomb. The capstone is partly displaced and the centre has been filled with stone. Evidence of the prehistoric field system is seen in the area of uncultivated land next to the gated road south-west of Treffynnon.

Trefin

Trefin is an attractive village on the coast road from St David's to Fishguard two and a half miles west of Mathry. The name means 'village on the rock outcrop'. It has a pub, the Ship and some pretty colour washed cottages on the main street. There is also a weaving centre, café and youth hostel. Modern development is mainly to the north or off the main street. There is a Baptist Chapel dating from 1843 and the older Calvinistic Methodist Chapel dating from 1786 but rebuilt in 1834 and restored 1936.

To the south of the village, just beyond the village sign is a footpath to Aber Felin, an 18th century corn mill which closed in 1918. The building, overlooking the sea, is in ruins but the millstones remain. It was the subject of the Welsh poem *Melin Trefin* by the Arch druid Crwys.

Treglemais

Treglemais is a small farming community on St David's Peninsular, off the A487 five miles north-east of St David's. The meaning of the name is uncertain. *Tre* is a dwelling place and there is a Glemais herd of cattle. Although small, there are some interesting farm buildings dating from the 18th century. Treglemais was formerly a manor of the Bishops of St David's, with records dating back to 1332.

A little under a mile from Treglemais is Llanhowell, with the pretty little 14th century church of St Hywel. The church consists of a nave, chancel and small north transept with squint passage and a bellcote. Heavily restored in the 19th and early 20th century the font dates from the 12th century. At the west end of the church is a 5th century stone inscribed 'RINACI NOMENA.' The stone was found at Carnhedryn Farm and installed in the chapel of ease of St James there. When St James was closed the stone was transferred to St Hywel's. The church of St James is now a private dwelling.

Trehilyn

Trehilyn is a tiny hamlet near Trefasser three miles west of Fishguard. Trehilyn means the settlement of Hilyn, a character in the *Mabinogion*. The farmhouse was the subject of a restoration television series with Griff Rhys Jones entitled *A Pembrokeshire Farmhouse*. The house is available for holiday rent. Beyond the house are the remains of Trehilyn Mill, a corn mill which operated until the 1930s.

Tufton

Tufton is a hamlet adjoining Henry's Moat on the B4329 two miles north-east of Puncheston at its junction with the road to Henry's Moat. The Tufton Arms, now closed was an old drovers' inn on the crossroads. An unusual building having white slate tiles as facing on the walls, the Tufton Arms doubled as an Irish pub in the film of Tony Hawkes' *Round Ireland with a Fridge*.

Siloh Independent Chapel dates from 1842 with a restoration in 1900.

Upton

Upton is a hamlet a mile east of Cosheston consisting of Upton Farm and Upton Castle and a few scattered cottages.

Upton Castle is a small, extensively altered, late 13th century castle, still occupied as a private home. Three original slender drum towers survive with evidence of a drawbridge and portcullis. Originally the castle was built by the Malefants, a Norman family who were knights of the Earl of Pembroke. The last Malefant was Henry whose daughter married Owen ap Griffith and their descendants adopted the surname of Bowen. In the 18th century the Upton estate was purchased by a Captain John Tasker, a local seafarer who

Upon Castle

had made his money in India, becoming captain of the East India Company ship Milford, based in Bombay. He died a bachelor and the estate passed to Revd Evans who had married his niece. In 1927 the estate was purchased by Stanley Neale who was responsible for the layout of the gardens. The castle has been modified and extended over the years with the residential part having been built in the 17th and 18th centuries with the addition of two further towers in the 19th century.

In the grounds is Upton Chapel dating from the 12th-13th century with limited 18th century renovation. The chapel consists of a nave, chancel and western bellcote and has a Norman font. There are a number of effigy monuments in the chapel, unidentified by Fenton but now one is attributed to William Malefant (1362) and two others to members of the family. In the north-east corner of the nave is a unique fist shaped taper holder protruding from the wall. The pulpit is from St Mary's Haverfordwest. The font is of the square Norman type and regarded as the finest example in Pembrokeshire.

The gardens are open to the public between 10.00 and 16.30 daily from April to October and extend to 35 acres.

Uzmaston

Uzmaston is a small village a mile and a half south-east of Haverfordwest on the Western Cleddau. The name derives from Osmond's Farm. Today there is a farm some concrete council houses and other cottages. The church of St Ismael dates from the 13th century and was granted in 1230 to the Knights of St John of Jerusalem at Slebech. The church, which was virtually rebuilt in 1870 and refurbished in the 1990s, is an unusual structure. The short chancel is offset and there is a north aisle and small south transept with squint. The 15th century tower adjoins the north aisle and entry is via a set of external stone steps to the first floor. It was probably taller prior to renovation. The church contains a number of monuments from Boulston church including a boulder in the churchyard with an inscription to the Wogans of Boulston. The church offers excellent views over the Western Cleddau.

William Roblin, a Pembrokeshire murderer of "intemperate passion" was hung on 23rd April, 1821, having been found guilty of shooting 23 year old William Davies on 18 August, 1820 at Deeplake, on the A40 main road, in the parish of Uzmaston. He was the last man to hang in the county.

Uzmaston church

Velindre (See Felindre Farchog)

Wallis

Wallis was first mentioned in 1572 as Walles, possibly referring to Wallis Rath. It is a hamlet near Ambleston of less than twenty houses. It faces Wallis Moor, a site of Special Scientific Interest because of its habitat and the range of its flora and fauna which includes the Marsh Fritillary butterfly, eleven species of dragonfly, orchids and otters which thrive in Spittal Brook.

Walton East

Walton East is believed to have been named after the Norman Walter de Wale who gifted it to the Knights of St John of Jerusalem at Slebech. Walton East is a small village situated one and a half miles north of Clarbeston Road. This pleasant agricultural village with plenty of green spaces is divided with the part, known as Little West, containing the Calvinistic Methodist Chapel built in 1878.

The church of St Mary is positioned next to a small village green. Described by Lewis in 1833 as "a very small rude edifice, consisting only of a nave", but the rebuilding of 1849-54 by Joseph Jenkins of

Haverfordwest has resulted in a nave, chancel, north porch and bellcote. A small vestry has also been added to the chancel.

A mile south-west of the village is Penty Park, former home of a branch of the Philipps family. An 18th century mansion restyled in the 19th century and recently renovated it is now owned by Direction Sportive and is available for hire and for specialist leadership and executive coaching programmes.

Half a mile north of the village is Scollock Rath, a large Iron Age defended enclosure, 380 feet in diameter with a second semi circular enclosure adjoining.

Walton West

Situated above Broad Haven, Walton West is a small scattered village with views over the coast. The church of All Saints was described by Lewis as "not entitled to architectural notice" and by the Revd Joseph Brown, in 1851, as being "in a very dilapidated and dangerous state, not fit for Divine Service". It was much rebuilt by Penson in 1854 when the tower was lowered and partly replaced by a gabled roof with bellcote, giving a most unusual outline. There is a second bellcote at the eastern end of the chapel.

Walton West

Walwyn's castle

Walwyn's Castle is a small village a mile and a half south-east of Broad
Haven. It takes its name from the Norman earthwork castle, built on
the site of an Iron Age enclosure. According to legend it was the burial
place of Sir Gawain, one of King Arthur's knights. Fenton asserts that
the body of Gualchmai, a cousin of Arthur and Regulus of Galway was
dug up here in the time of William the Conqueror. A man of large
stature, he was driven out of Ireland and died on the coast in a
shipwreck and buried here. Built within the Iron Age enclosure, the
Norman castle occupies a promontory above the valley and consisted
of an outer bailey, upper bailey, lower bailey and motte. Despite being
constructed of wood rather than stone, it remained in use for some
considerable time, with Guy de Bryan born here in 1254 and his son,
also Guy in 1289. The de Bryans were Barons of Castle Walwyn and
had the subsidiary castles of Dale and Benton, both of which were of
stone. This may be explained by the fact that the de Bryans' main seat
was at Laugharne in Carmarthenshire. The earthworks are immediately
south of the church and today stand above a small reservoir.

The church of St James the Great stands on raised ground giving
extensive views across the south-west of the county. The west tower
dates from the late 14th to early 15th century though, like the rest of
the church, it underwent extensive renovation in the late 19th century.
There is a nave, chancel and north porch with additional extensions to
the chancel. Unusually, the main door has glass.

1000 yards downstream from Walwyn's Castle is Syke Rath, an Iron
Age inland promontory fort, near Wood Farm, accessible by footpath
from Syke Farm.

Warren

Warren is an ancient parish on the Castlemartin Peninsular, a mile east
of the village of Castlemartin. The name suggests that rabbits were
bred there. In 1833 the population was just 169 and with the
Castlemartin Ranges the civil population is small. The church of St
Mary however serves as a multi-denominational place of worship for
the forces serving at the base.

The church dates from 1290 and consists of a nave, chancel, south
transept and porch and a west tower, unusually for Pembrokeshire,
topped with a stone spire. A north aisle was demolished in 1770
because of damp though the outline of the arches can still be seen. The
guide to the church suggests that the spire was wooden and replaced

in 1855, but Lewis described it as a stone spire in 1833. The church was refurbished in 1855 at the expense of Lord Cawdor with the architect David Brandon, who was also responsible for Hensol Castle in Glamorgan and Badminton House. In the 1970s the church was again in a state of disrepair and was to be closed. The Warren Church Trust was formed in 1986 and funding for the restoration was raised by the British and German troops based at the range. The font cover and altar table were made in Germany and donated by the West German government. The organ dates from 1842 and originally belonged to the composer Felix Mendelssohn. It was moved to Warren and restored in 1988. The window by the organ is in memory of Major General Sir Edmund Leach who lived at nearby Corston House, while the memorial nearby to his son Brigadier General Henry Leach, organiser of the 1919 London Peace March, is thought to be by Eric Gill.

In the churchyard is a wheel cross, of 19th century construction but on a medieval base.

Opposite the church is Warren Farm dating from the 18th century with a massive chimney. A similarly large chimney is a feature of the 18th century Cold Comfort Cottages 500 yards to the north-west.

At the side of the road, 370 yards to the north-west, hidden in undergrowth is a well with stone canopy.

Waterston

Waterston is a village between Milford Haven and Neyland adjoining the giant Dragon liquefied natural gas plant. The village has some attractive older properties including the former Three Crowns, on the crossroads. There is some new housing including retired accommodation to the west and an industrial area. The Waterston Wesleyan Methodist Church built in 1836 stands at the entrance to the gas terminal.

1000 yards north-east of the village is Scoveton Fort. Now tree clad the hexagonal Victorian fort was designed as one of a series of forts to protect the Haven. It was the only inland fort and built on high ground, designed for a garrison of 128 men manning 32 guns it was never manned on a permanent basis. It was used for training in World War I and as a munitions store ahead of D Day. Now derelict and dangerous to enter it is a massive structure, some 330 yards across, with each of the six sides measuring 130 yards, but hardly noticeable from the road.

Welsh Hook
Welsh Hook is a small village a mile and a half north-west of Wolfscastle. The narrow two arched bridge is the first to cross the Western Cleddau as a river rather than a stream. Nearby is the attractive old corn mill and the little church of St Lawrence, with its nave, chancel and double bellcote. Stone Hall Mansion was in use as a hotel and restaurant, though it had just four bedrooms. One of the homes of the Wogan family, the house dates back 600 years though was much altered in the 18th and 19th centuries. Surrounding the Mansion is an arboretum.

West Williamston
Situated a little over a mile south-west of Cresswell Quay, between the Cresswell and Carew rivers, West Williamston is a quiet hamlet of old farm buildings and cottages on narrow lanes. The area to the west was the subject of extensive limestone quarrying in the 18th and 19th centuries and there are the remains of limekilns to the north of Rosemary Lane. Williamston Park is now a National Trust Woodland.

Whitchurch
Whitchurch is a small village three quarters of a mile north of Solva. Open green spaces and little modern development make this an appealing rural village. The church of St David is a substantial building with nave, chancel, north transept and western bellcote and retains much medieval fabric. It was a chapelry of the cathedral until the later medieval period when it became a parish. The Welsh name for the village is Tregroes, or 'settlement of the cross' and inside the church gate is a stone thought to be the upright of an ancient cross and known as Maen Dewi. The old parish included Solva, which explains the size of the church.

Williamston
Williamston is an estate, formerly the residence of the Bowen family, just south of Roose Ferry Road leading from Houghton. The estate passed through marriage to the Phillips family who changed the spelling to Philipps and again through marriage to the Scourfield family. The gardens were quite elaborate with the entrance carriageway passing between two lakes. In 1908 Williamston was the scene of a meeting of the Pembrokeshire Automobile Club of which Sir Owen Henry Philipps Scourfield was president. The club's annual hill

climb was held on the estate. Sir Owen died childless and, in 1922, the estate was purchased by a Mr Dixon whose family still own the farm. The Victorian house is now a nursing home. Fenton surmises that the house was built as an alternative to the 13th century Benton Castle, a mile to the east. Benton, originally a subsidiary of Walwyn's Castle has been restored and is now a private home.

Wisemans Bridge

Wiseman's Bridge is a hamlet on the coast east of Saundersfoot. The bridge crosses the Rath Fehan stream and was first mentioned in 1598, though the first bridge is probably earlier as the Wisemans are listed in the parish of St Issels in the 14th century.

The beach is a mixture of sand and rocks and there is the Wisemans Bridge Inn and a number of caravan sites.

It is possible to walk to Saundersfoot through a tunnel that used to carry coal for shipping from Saundersfoot Harbour.

Wiston (Welsh Castell Gwys)

Wiston is a small village north of the A40 between Narberth and Haverfordwest. Houses are well set back from the road with limited development of new housing to the west. Formerly a borough, the village, although much reduced in population, retained its mayor into the 19th century and had a fair on November 8th annually.

At the centre of the village is the church of St Mary, Wiston Castle and Wiston Manor.

Founded by Wizo the Fleming, some time around 1112, Wiston was once a thriving borough. According to Fenton, Wizo's grandson was Sir Philip Gwys and his daughter and heiress married Gwgan ap Bleddyn. The family adopted the Anglicized form of Wogan and the Wogans of Wiston played an important part in the life of Pembrokeshire until 1794 when the estate was sold to John Campbell, Lord Cawdor. Sir John Wogan of Wiston married Joan Picton and thus inherited the Picton estate.

Wizo built the castle, which is possibly the best preserved motte and bailey castle in Wales on the site of an Iron Age enclosure. It was taken by the sons of Gruffydd ap Rhys in 1147 and again in 1193 and in 1220 by Llewellyn the Great. It was after Llewellyn's attack that the borough started to decline, but it is thought that the stonework surviving on the motte dates from work carried out by the Earl of Pembroke after its recapture. The motte is some 24 feet high with the stone defences above it having a diameter of 58 feet. The bailey occupies an area of nearly 14000 square yards. There is no evidence of any stonework on the walls of the bailey. In the 18th century a new Manor House was built and incorporated the castle as a feature in the gardens. The castle is in the care of Cadw and admission, 10.00-16.00 daily, is free

The church of St Mary Magdalene was built by Wizo and gifted to the Priory at Worcester. In 1175 it was granted to the Knights of St John of Jerusalem at Slebech at a rent of 11 marks. The church consists of a nave, chancel and four storey west tower with entry via a north porch.

Wolfscastle

Wolfscastle and its accompanying hamlet Ford lie on the A40, seven miles north of Haverfordwest, at the confluence of the Western Cleddau and the Afon Anghof (called the Sealy by Fenton). The village is named after the Norman motte and bailey castle that stands between the two rivers on the eastern side of the A40. It is said that the last wolf in Wales was killed here. Alternatively the name derives from the Norman Ulfa who established the motte and bailey castle.

Away from the busy A40, the village, built on a hill, is picturesque with plenty of green space. The Wolfscastle Country House Hotel is in the former rectory.

The church of St Margaret lies to the south of the village of Ford on the A40. It is a simple single cell building with a porch, west door and bellcote. It was built in 1627 by Margaret Symmons of Puncheston to provide church services for her tenants. It was renovated in the latter part of the 18th century.

Fenton, on his tour, noted the site of a Roman villa, in a field 800 yards west of Ford, in the corner of the field adjoining the settlement, marked on the OS map. His findings were dismissed for nearly 200 years as it was believed that the Romans had never been established so far west. In 2003 however an archaeological dig confirmed Fenton's findings.

Ford Camp, marked Settlement on the map, lies 110 yards from the site of the villa and is circular with a diameter of 140 feet. There is evidence of four buildings but the dating of the camp is uncertain and may post-date the villa.

Just under a mile north-east of Wolfscastle is Sealyham Mansion. Established by the Tucker family, the mansion was built by Admiral

Thomas Tucker in the 18th century. The first Tucker was Sir William who was seneschal to Hugh de Lacy, Constable of Chester in the 12th century. A marriage linked the Tuckers with the Edwardes family of Treffgarne and Captain Jack Edwardes developed the Sealyham Terrier breed here in the early 19th century. The mansion was used as a Tuberculosis hospital from 1923 but is now the centre of Sealyham Activity Centre, offering activity courses and days for children.

Wolfscastle lies in the parish of St Dogwells and the parish church lies a little under a mile from the village, across the river from Sealyham Mansion. Parts of the church date back to the 12th century with a south aisle added in the 15th-16th century. It has a double bellcote, with an external bell pull and entrance is through the southern porch. It is dedicated to St Dogfael though there are other spellings, including Dogmael and Dogwell. The Welsh name is Llantydewi, recognizing that the church was given to St David's in the 13th century.

In the churchyard is the Hogtivis Stone inscribed 'HOGTIVIS FILI/ DEMETI' in Latin and 'OGTENLO' in Ogham. Thought to be 6th century, the stone was discovered in 1875 being used as a gatepost at Little Treffgarne. Standing 6ft 4 inches high, the stone is set to the west of the church.

Woodstock

Woodstock is a small farming community above the western shore of Llys y Frân Reservoir. Its skyline is dominated by the radio and digital television transmitter which broadcasts to the bulk of Pembrokeshire. On land 614 feet above sea level, the mast is 509 feet high.

There has been some expansion on the B4329 near the Calvinistic Methodist Chapel on the cross roads. The chapel was established in 1754.

Yerbiston

Yerbiston now consists of a farm and the converted church of St Lawrence, on a country road four and a half miles south-west of Narberth. An unusual feature of the church is the 16th century belfry which takes the form of a mini-tower built above the west wall.

On the nearby main A4075 is Yerbiston Gate Farm Shop and to the north at Yerbiston Mountain, a farm and caravan centre.

Sources and further reading

Bibliography

Archaeologia Cambrensis
Baring-Gould, S. *The Lives of the British Saints*, 1911
Cambrensis, Giraldus. *Itinerarium Kambriae and Descriptio Kambriae*
Fenton, Richard. *A Historical Tour Through Pembrokeshire*, 1810
Hall, Mrs S.C. *Book of South Wales, the Wye and the Coast*, 1863
Heath Malkin, Benjamin. *The Scenery Antiquities and Biographies of South Wales*, 1804
Hewlett Edwards, Emily. *Castles and Strongholds of Pembrokeshire*, 1909
Lewis, Samuel. *A Topographical Dictionary of Wales*, 1835
Mirehouse, Mary Beatrice. *South Pembrokeshire*, 1910
Morgan, Mary. *A Tour to Milford Haven in the Year 1791*
Owen, George. *The Description of Penbrockshire*, 1603
Rees, Thomas. *The beauties of England and Wales: or, Delineations, topographical, histrical, and descriptive, of each county*, 1815
The Royal Commission on the Ancient and Historical Monuments and Constructions in Wales and Monmouthshire, *Inventory Vol VII County of Pembroke*, 1925
Sikes, Wirt. *British Goblins Welsh Folk-lore, Fairy Mythology, Legends and Traditions*, 1880
Timmins, H. Thornhill. *Nooks and Corners of Pembrokeshire*, 1895

Online resources

The History of Parliament Online
www.historyofparliamentonline.org
Dyfed Archaeological Trust
www.archaeologists.net/ro/49-dyfed-archaeological-trust
Welsh Biography Online (National Library of Wales)
www.coflein.gov.uk